Mrs. M. W. Harrington
Sept. 21st 1874

THE

AMATEUR ACTOR

A Collection of

PLAYS FOR SCHOOL AND HOME

BY

W. H. VENABLE,

Author of "June on the Miami, and other Poems;" "A School History of the United States," etc.

WILSON, HINKLE & CO.,

137 WALNUT STREET, CINCINNATI.

28 BOND STREET, NEW YORK.

ELECTROTYPED AT THE FRANKLIN TYPE FOUNDRY, CINCINNATI.

PREFACE.

This volume contains twenty-three dramatic pieces, the greater number of which are taken from the writings of standard authors. The selections are adapted for easy representation as school or parlor plays, and although some of them will admit of ambitious acting and much spectacular display, none will prove impracticable on the amateur stage. The humorous element predominates in the book, yet few of the scenes are what, in theatrical phrase, is termed 'broad.' The performers of the comic parts will be obliged to depend, for applause, upon the wit of the speeches, rather than upon vulgar *gags* or senseless buffoonery. One rollicking pantomime is introduced for the sake of variety, and—at the other extreme—one little tragedy.

The editor has made no alterations in the text of authors copied from, excepting such as the nature of the compilation imperatively required, namely, large omissions, occasional transpositions, and now and then the substitution of different phraseology for profane or otherwise objectionable epithets and expressions. In some cases, dramatic coherence demanded the addition of a few words or lines; and these interpolated passages are invariably denoted by half-quotation marks.

In preparing stage directions and description of costume, recourse was had to various editions of acting plays, and to the taste and judgment of several persons experienced in the management of private theatricals.

The Introduction contains plain and full directions for making all necessary preparations to insure the success of ordinary amateur plays. The reader may rest assured that what is therein described and recommended can be, and, in fact, has been realized by actual trial.

Mr. Farny's very suggestive designs, which have received remarkably fair treatment at the hands of the engraver, speak for themselves, and can not fail to be regarded as a recommendation of the volume. W. H. V.

April 2, 1874.

CONTENTS.

Introduction.

The Stage and Proscenium.

MOST dramas, being designed for theatrical representation, require, for their proper performance, a stage, with proscenium and curtains. The *stage* is simply an elevated platform, twelve feet or more long, by eight or more wide, the size depending upon that of the audience-room. A short distance back on the stage the *proscenium* is erected, affording support to the curtain, and concealing the preparations of actors from the gaze of spectators. The proscenium consists of a light, strong, wooden frame, forming, with the plane of the floor, an area nearly square, and of a size to correspond with the dimensions of the stage. The space between the sides of the proscenium and the walls of the audience-room is generally draped with muslin, of a rich maroon-color, gathered in vertical folds. So also is the space between the top of the proscenium and the ceiling of the room.

The proscenium may be ornamented according to taste, either by gilding, painting, papering; or by the use of chains and festoons of evergreen; flags; and wreaths of flowers. The surface of the stage should be carpeted, or else painted green. The space in front, between the foot-lights and the floor, should be rendered sightly with paint, or hangings of some kind. Excessive decoration is to be avoided, since it defeats the true purpose of all adornment—the gratification of good taste.

The Curtain.

The proper material for a stage curtain is green baize. There are two methods of working the ordinary drop-curtain: first, by means of a roller and cords after the manner of an awning, or a window-shade; and, second, as illustrated in the accompanying diagram. Several rows of small brass rings are sewed to strips of tape fastened to the back of the curtain. Cords, tied to a weight-pole at the bottom of the curtain, run through the rings to the top, and passing over pulleys, descend to one side of the stage, and afford a convenient means of lifting and

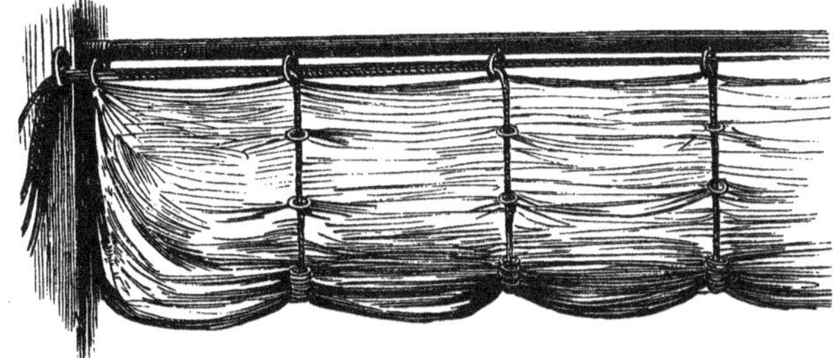

lowering the curtain. Of course the curtain must be made fast to the top of the proscenium frame.

The common draw-curtain, consisting of two pieces, is suspended by rings sliding on a smooth rod or wire, and is easily worked from one side with strong cords, as represented in the cut. The draw-

curtain is very graceful when well managed, but requires rather more material in the making than the *drop*, as it should hang in ample folds.

Scenery.

Behind the proscenium and curtain is the acting stage with its scenery and appointments. On either side of the stage are the *entrances*—spaces from two to three feet wide—separated from one another by *wings*, or high rectangular screens. The number of entrances depends upon the depth of the stage; but rarely exceeds two in an amateur play-house.

Two principal sorts of *scenes* are used, *side-scenes*, or wings, and back-scenes. Narrow horizontal *hanging-scenes*, or *soffits*, are used to screen the space over the stage.

"Back-scenes are of two kinds, viz.: *rolling-scenes*, which are let down from above, and *flats*, which are formed of two sliding-scenes strained upon framing, like the wings, and meeting each other and uniting in the center. These are employed when what are termed *practicable* scenes are required; that is, doors, windows, etc., which admit of being used as real doors, etc., or else when there is occasion that the 'flat' should suddenly open and discover another scene behind it.

"In addition to these there are what are termed *open* flats, which are scenes cut out in places so that both the background is seen and the actors can pass through them. They are commonly used for the representation of groves or forests, but sometimes for interiors with open arches. There are, besides, what are technically known as *set-pieces*—narrow scenes placed obliquely on one side of the stage when it is wanted to show a cottage or corner of a house with a *practicable* door in it."

Rolling-scenes are recommended for the amateur theater. They are raised and lowered like the drop-curtain, or even like an ordinary wall-map. Wings and flats may be made by stretching muslin or strong paper over stout wooden frames of the proper size. The muslin surface must be primed with a coat of sized whitening, which, when dry, leaves the cloth ready for the artist's design.

Scene-painting is an art which requires time, judgment, and skill. Only the simplest subjects should be attempted by the amateur. The design is first sketched lightly in charcoal. Suitable pictures may sometimes be selected from books, or drawn on a small surface and then enlarged to the scale required on the scene by a process often used in map-drawing. The small picture must be of the shape required on the canvas. It is first divided into a number of equal spaces by means of a pencil and dividers. The canvas to which it is to be transferred is also divided by faint tracings, into the same number of similar spaces. The corresponding spaces in the two surfaces are numbered alike. Now, with the small copy in hand, it is easy to outline on the large surface, within each numbered space, what is represented within the corresponding space of the small copy.

The colors used in scene-painting are ground in water and mixed with thin size. The predominating hues should be such as will harmonize with the dresses of the actors. There should be little attempt at perspective effect in back-scenes unless the depth of the stage is considerable.

Substitutes for Painted Scenery.

When painted scenery can not be provided, the stage may be hung about with green, brown, or claret-colored curtains of muslin, or, better, of woolen. These may be made to part at points convenient for

entrance and exit. Side screens, covered with wall-paper and attached by hinges to the sides of the stage, as shown in the picture, answer the purpose of wings. If, in addition to these, two large, movable, folding screens be set upon the back of the stage, a very good representation of a room may be made, with practicable doors on every side.

It was the custom, at and before the time of Shakespeare (1564–1626), to indicate to the spectators the place of action, by hanging conspicuously, at the back of the stage, a placard briefly describing the scene to be imagined. This may be done in the amateur theater. See the accompanying cut.

Lighting the Stage.

Whenever an evening performance is given, provision should be made for lighting the stage, either by means of gas, oil, or candles. If kerosene or coal-oil is used, it should be only in safety-lamps.

Extreme caution and care must be taken to avoid the possibility of accidents by fire. To this end every burner used about the stage should be surrounded by a glass chimney or globe, and further protected by guards of wire.

Foot-lights are indispensable. They are placed in a row across the front of the stage, and supplied with polished reflectors, which throw the light strongly upon the actors. Head-lights are also of great advantage; and a few side-lights are necessary to prevent the shadows of the actors from being visible on the wings. One great advantage of gas-light is that it can be so readily increased or diminished at pleasure.

When an intense light is required, as in the illumination of tableaux, magnesium strips or wires can be burned in front of a reflector at the side of the stage, behind the wings. Magnesium may be obtained in any large city.

"To produce darkness, a thick piece of crape doubled may be fixed in a frame and interposed between the foot-lights and the stage, and lamp-blacked glasses should be fitted on to the lights behind." Different colored illuminations are effected by placing different colored glass-globes upon the side lamps; or by the use of the apparatus known as the *magnesium lantern*, consisting of a tin box with slides of colored glass. The burning of chemical mixtures for illuminating the stage is scarcely to be recommended, unless the theater be very large, and well-ventilated.

In order to give the light upon the stage sufficient brilliancy, it will sometimes be necessary to lower that in the auditorium.

Stage Effects.

Theatrical lightning is produced by throwing through a jet of flame a pinch of lycopodium, or of fine gunpowder mixed with a little sulphur. Thunder is imitated by shaking a long sheet of tin or iron, or by rolling a heavy ball on the floor. The sound of rain is simulated by causing a quantity of dried peas to roll from end to end of a long narrow box, having the bottom studded with small wooden pegs; or by throwing handfuls of dried peas against a surface of paper stretched tightly on a frame. The sound of distant artillery is imitated by tapping on a large drum. The crash of breaking windows, or the like, is made by dashing to the floor a closed basket containing several pieces of tin.

Stage Terms and Directions.

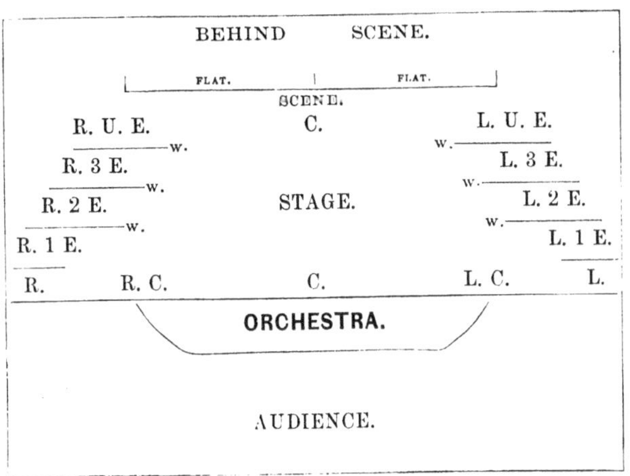

R. means Right; L., Left; C., Center; R. C., Right Center; L. C., Left Center; R. 1 E., Right First Entrance; L. 2 E., Left Second Entrance; R. U. E., Right Upper Entrance; W., Wing.

The actor is supposed to face the audience. The Right and the Left Upper Entrance are always next to the back scene, wherever that may be. The number of entrances depends upon the depth of the stage. *To go up* is to approach the back scene; *to come down* is to move toward the foot-lights.

Properties and Accessories.

Under the head of properties are included many articles used by actors, independently of scenery and costumes, such as furniture, arms, banners, agricultural implements, domestic utensils, thrones, altars, crowns, and wands. With a little ingenuity the amateur can contrive, at trifling cost, such necessary articles as are not obtainable ready-made. Shields, breast-plates, and the simpler forms of helmets and crowns, may be cut out of strong pasteboard, and covered with tin-foil, gilt paper, or Dutch metal. Swords, spears, and battle-axes may be clipped out of tin. Long broom handles or rollers for window-shades serve as spear-shafts and supports for banners. Scepters and wands are made of wood, covered with bronze or silver.

Wings for fairies and elves are formed of gauze or bobinet stretched over skeletons of wire. Stars and spangles may be cut from silver paper, and different colored foil. Jewels are represented by glittering steel and glass. Imitation gold and silver lace and fringe may be had at fancy stores. Paint, artificial flowers, tissue paper, and, in short, all varieties of gay and gaudy material, are employed in producing theatrical effects. But these are to be used with taste and discretion. A meaningless profusion of tinseled properties, though it may delight the vulgar, "can not but make the judicious grieve."

Costume.

"Costume," says Benjamin Clayton, "is the observance of propriety in regard to the person or thing represented, so that the scene of action, the habits, arms, proportions, etc., are properly imitated. The peculiarities of form, physiognomy, complexion, dress, ornaments, etc., should be all conformable to the period and country in which the scene is laid. The rules of costume would be violated by the introduction of one or more figures arrayed in the scanty raiment of the Hindoos into a scene in Siberia; by the representation of American Indians in turbans and top-boots; or by Romans dressed in tail-coats and peg-tops, serving cannon at the siege of Carthage."

Amateur players often violate the proprieties of costume from an inordinate desire to make a display at all events. True, one object of theatrical representations is picturesque and showy effect, but a higher object is "to hold the mirror up to nature" and truth. The actor's dress and appurtenances should accord with historical probability, and the particular character of the person represented. When a piece requiring peculiar and varied costume is to be brought out, the performers should consult together, and agree as to the dress and ornaments that each should adopt. This is extremely necessary, in order to avoid the juxtaposition, on the stage, of inharmonious colors. Any dressmaker or milliner knows that certain colors will not go well together. The actor who is ambitious to discover the foundations of the costumer's art will study the philosophy of color, and learn the laws of contrast, complement, and blending.* Green and red may always be exhibited side by side, also yellow and violet, orange and blue, and like complementary hues. The colors in contrast should be of the same intensity.

Those who have access to a city may hire "character dresses," armor, wigs, etc., at the costumer's or from the theaters. When this is not practicable, recourse must be had to home skill and invention. Some persons have a knack of making much of little wardrobe, and are able, with a few shawls, fleshings, scarfs, and cast-aside silken garments, to devise a great variety of costume suitable for the stage. Furs, velvets, glazed calico, ladies' "switches," plumes, beads, fringe, lace, and spangles may be made to produce many pleasing effects.

Persons unaccustomed to wearing fancy dresses, armor, swords, long cloaks, sweeping trains, and the like, will find it no light task to appear easy and graceful in the management of these articles. For

*See M. E. Chevreul's Laws of Contrast of Color.

this reason dress rehearsals are quite indispensable. A splendid costume awkwardly worn is sure to subject the wearer to disagreeable criticism.

Making Up the Face.

The actor's head and face must sometimes be dressed and painted to imitate the characteristic features of the person represented. False hair, beards, and mustaches, often disguise the face effectually, and change its aspect in many ways. The safest and simplest coloring materials for the face are common flour, charcoal, and rouge. Burnt cork is used to blacken the face for negro characters. India ink, applied with a camel's hair brush, is used to represent wrinkles. A comic expression is produced upon the face by touching the nose and the cheek-bones with rouge, or, by tracing in paint, the lines which the actor's countenance assumes when laughing. Toilet powder is employed to give whiteness to the forehead, neck, and arms. A too lavish use of powder and paint must be avoided, especially if the stage be small and close to the audience.

The Orchestra.

Instrumental music should be provided as a prelude and accompaniment of every dramatic performance. A full orchestra is desirable; but where this can not be secured, the company must obtain the best substitute at their command, be it a string band, a piano, a melodeon, or even a single violin.

The Dramatic Company.

The ladies and gentlemen who volunteer to take part in a play, whether they be members of a school, a social party, a literary society, or a regular dramatic club, must expect to make many mutual concessions, and to find constant occasion for prudence, self-denial, good humor, patience, and politeness. The green-room affords an excellent school for conduct.

The first thing for the considerate amateur to remember is, that he or she is but an individual member of a company designed to give pleasure by harmonious cöoperation. Each performer must subordinate his personality to the general purpose of the company. Let no vulgar ambition to exhibit self, at the expense of others, or at the sacrifice of dramatic propriety, lead any actor to make himself troublesome or ridiculous. It too often happens, in dramatic societies, that some irrepressible member, more distinguished by conceit than ability, checks the ardor, and destroys the temper of his associates, for want of a broad hint that he is obtrusive and vain. This paragraph is written for that man, in behalf of his fellow-actors.

The Manager.

The company should select for their manager a person who has some practical knowledge of the stage, and one whom they are willing to obey implicitly in all matters pertaining to their respective parts. The manager's decision must silence all dissenting voices. His word is stage law. A unified plan is absolutely essential to success in producing a play. The regulations of first-class theaters are exceedingly stringent. Tyros must not chafe under what may seem to them needlessly arbitrary restrictions. The manager can scarcely be too strict. It is his duty to select plays and assign the parts, to superintend rehearsals, to drill the actors in their speech and action, to arrange them in the proper manner on the stage, to advise concerning scenery, costume, and properties.

Selecting Plays to Act.

For a school exhibition, or a lyceum entertainment, of which dramatic performances form but a part of the exercises, it is not well to attempt more than one or two dress pieces, and they should be short. One serious act or scene, from some standard tragedy or high comedy, and one elegant comic selection, carefully prepared, will give more satisfaction than half a dozen miscellaneous scenes imperfectly gotten up. Of course the selections made must be adapted to the taste, comprehension, and dramatic ability of the performers. The manager casts the play according to his best judgment, assigning to each actor his rôle or character to study. It is a very excellent plan for the manager to read the play aloud to the company, with such hints, comments, and explanations as he may deem useful. "No committing of the piece to memory will be of service," says Göethe, "if the actor have not, in the first place, penetrated into the sense and spirit of his author; the mere letter will avail him nothing."

Memorizing Plays.

Each actor should, if possible, commit to memory the entire play, for a perfect comprehension of the several parts depends upon an accurate knowledge of the whole. By all means be familiar with the language of your own rôle. Learn the exact text of your part, as printed, and adhere to it with scrupulous care. Do not alter or omit a single word.

Rehearsals.

As soon as a play has been cast, the actors should commence book rehearsals, that is, they should read and study the piece in common, that they may catch the spirit of it, and learn its peculiar difficulties. Then should follow several stage rehearsals without aid from the book. These rehearsals should be repeated until every actor becomes, in professional phrase, *dead perfect* in his part. All the actors must be present at every rehearsal. The company should observe the utmost order, and give the closest attention to the instructions of the manager. The great German poet, Göethe, who was himself a dramatic author, and had much practical experience as a manager, advises players "that throughout the whole of their preparations, the posture and action, as they are intended ultimately to appear, should always be combined with the words, and thus the whole be mechanically united by habit. In rehearsing a tragedy, especially, no common movement with the hands should be allowed."

The habit most difficult for amateurs to acquire is that of speaking loud enough to be heard anywhere in the auditorium. This habit must be established at the rehearsals. The manager may take his seat at the corner of the room remotest from the stage, and, whenever he fails to hear what an actor is saying, he should interrupt the speech and require it to be repeated.

One or two dress-rehearsals should be had before the final public performance of a play. These should be attended by the prompter, whose duty it is to remain at the right wing with a printed copy of the play, and to prompt the players whenever they require his assistance.

The Art of Acting.

Our remarks on the art of acting will necessarily be general. The purpose of dramatic performance is the life-like representation, to the eye and the ear, of events, passions, humors, and ideas. Every actor personates an imaginary being in whom he must sink his own individuality. He must dress, move, speak, think, and feel, as nearly as possible, as he supposes the character he represents would do. He must imagine that he *is* that character, and that his fellow-actors are what they seem to be. To do this is to appear natural on the stage, and to appear natural is the perfection of dramatic art.

There are a few grand requisites to success in any line of stage playing,—good sense, good articulation, a sufficiently strong voice, a firm step, and the ability to stand still. To those requisites add taste, vivacity, gracefulness, and a degree of enthusiasm, and we have mentioned most of the qualities of a good actor.

The best general directions ever written on the subject of acting are contained in

Hamlet's Advice to the Players.

Hamlet. Speak the speech, I pray you, as I pronounced it to you, trippingly on the tongue; but if you mouth it, as many of your players do, I had as lief the town-crier spoke my lines. Nor do not saw the air too much with your hand, thus; but use all gently: for in the very torrent, tempest, and, as I may say, the whirlwind of passion, you must acquire and beget a temperance, that may give it smoothness. Oh, it offends me to the soul to hear a robustious, periwig-pated fellow tear a passion to tatters, to very rags, to split the ears of the groundlings; who, for the most part, are capable of nothing but inexplicable dumb shows and noise: I would have such a fellow whipped for o'erdoing Termagant; it outherods Herod. Pray you avoid it.

First Player. I warrant, your honor.

Hamlet. Be not too tame, neither, but let your own discretion be your tutor: suit the action to the word, the word to the action; with this special observance, that you o'erstep not the modesty of nature; for anything so overdone is from the purpose of playing, whose end, both at the first and now, was, and is, to hold, as 't were, the mirror up to nature; to show virtue her own feature, scorn her own image, and the very age and body of the time his form and pressure. Now, this overdone, or come tardy off, though it make the unskillful laugh, can not but make the judicious grieve; the censure of which one must, in your allowance, o'erweigh a whole theater of others.

Oh, there be players that I have seen play—and heard others praise, and that highly—not to speak it profanely, that, neither having the accent of Christians, nor the gait of Christian, Pagan, nor Turk, have so strutted and bellowed, that I have thought some of Nature's journeymen had made men, and not made them well, they imitated humanity so abominably.

First Player. I hope we have reformed that indifferently with us.

Hamlet. Oh, reform it altogether. And let those that play your clowns speak no more than is set down for them. For there be of them that will themselves laugh, to set on some quantity of barren spectators to laugh too; though, in the meantime, some necessary question of the play be then to be considered: that 's villainous, and shows a most pitiful ambition in the fool that uses it. Go, make you ready.

OBERON AND TITANIA.

A Fairy Drama.

From Shakespeare's Midsummer Night's Dream.

PERSONS REPRESENTED.

OBERON, *king of the fairies.*
TITANIA, *queen of the fairies.*
PUCK, *or Robin-Goodfellow, a fairy.*
NICK BOTTOM, *a weaver of Athens.*
PEAS-BLOSSOM, COBWEB, MOTE, MUSTARD-SEED, *fairies.*
OTHER FAIRIES, *in attendance upon Oberon and Titania.*

SCENE I:—*A wood near Athens. Enter* OBERON, R., *at one door, with his Train; and* TITANIA, L., *at another, with hers.*

Ober. Ill met by moonlight, proud Titania
Tit. What, jealous Oberon! Fairies, skip hence.
Ober. Tarry, rash wanton; am not I thy lord?
Tit. Then, I must be thy lady; but I know
When thou hast stol'n away from Fairy-land,
And in the shape of Corin sat all day,
Playing on pipes of corn, and versing love
To amorous Phillida. Why art thou here,
Come from the farthest steep of India,
But that, forsooth, the bouncing Amazon,
Your buskin'd mistress, and your warrior love,
To Theseus must be wedded?
Ober. How canst thou thus, for shame, Titania,
Glance at my credit with Hippolyta,
Knowing I know thy love to Theseus?
Didst thou not lead him through the glimmering night,
And make him with fair Ægle break his faith,
With Ariadne, and Antiopa?
Tit. These are the forgeries of jealousy:
And never, since the middle Summer's spring,
Met we on hill, in dale, forest, or mead,
By paved fountain, or by rushy brook,
Or on the beached margent of the sea,
To dance our ringlets to the whistling wind,
But with thy brawls thou hast disturbed our sport.

Therefore the winds, piping to us in vain,
As in revenge, have suck'd up from the sea
Contagious fogs; which, falling in the land,
Have every petty river made so proud,
That they have overborne their continents:
The ox hath therefore stretched his yoke in vain,
The plowman lost his sweat; and the green corn
Hath rotted, ere his youth attain'd a beard:
The fold stands empty in the drowned field;
And crows are fatted with the murrain flock:
And Nine Men's Morris is fill'd up with mud;
And the quaint mazes in the wanton green,
For lack of tread are undistinguishable:
The human mortals want their Winter here,
No night is now with hymn or carol blest:—
Therefore the moon, the governess of floods,
Pale in her anger, washes all the air,
That rheumatic diseases do abound:
And thorough this distemperature, we see
The seasons alter: hoary-headed frosts
Fall in the fresh lap of the crimson rose;
And on old Hyems' thin, and icy crown,
An odorous chaplet of sweet summer buds
Is, as in mockery, set. The Spring, the Summer,
The childing Autumn, angry Winter, change
Their wonted liveries; and the 'mazed world,
By their increase, now knows not which is which.
And this same progeny of evils comes
From our debate, from our dissension:
We are their parents and original. [*Crosses to* R.

Ober. Do you amend it, then: it lies in you.
Why should Titiania cross her Oberon?
I do but beg a little changeling boy
To be my henchman.

Tit. Set your heart at rest:
The Fairy-land buys not the child of me.
His mother was a vot'ress of my order;
And in the spiced Indian air, by night,
Full often hath she gossip'd by my side,
And sat with me on Neptune's yellow sands,
Marking th' embarked traders on the flood;
And for her sake I do rear up her boy;
[*Goes up* C.
And for her sake I will not part with him.

Ober. How long within this wood intend you stay?

Tit. Perchance, till after Theseus' wedding-day.
If you will patiently dance in our round,
And see our moonlight revels, go with us;
If not, shun me, and I will spare your haunts.

Ober. Give me that boy, and I will go with thee.

Tit. Not for thy fairy kingdom.—Fairies, away!
We shall chide downright, if I longer stay.
[*Music.* FAIRIES *dance off.* *Exit* TITANIA.

Ober. (R.) Well, go thy way: thou shalt not from this grove,
Till I torment thee for this injury.—
My gentle Puck, come hither. [*Enter* PUCK, L. 2 E.
Thou rememb'rest
Since once I sat upon a promontory,
And heard a mermaid, on a dolphin's back,

Uttering such dulcet and harmonious breath,
That the rude sea grew civil at her song,
And certain stars shot madly from their spheres,
To hear the sea-maid's music.

Puck. (L. C.) I remember.

Ober. That very time I saw (but thou could'st not),
Flying between the cold moon and the Earth,
Cupid, all arm'd: a certain aim he took
At a fair vestal throned by the West,
And loosed his love-shaft smartly from his bow,
As it should pierce a hundred thousand hearts:
But I might see young Cupid's fiery shaft
Quenched in the chaste beams of the wat'ry moon,
And the imperial vot'ress passed on,
In maiden meditation, fancy-free.
Yet marked I where the bolt of Cupid fell:
It fell upon a little western flower,
Before milk-white, now purple with love's wound;
And maidens call it Love-in-idleness.
Fetch me that flower; the herb I showed thee once:
The juice of it, on sleeping eyelids laid,
Will make or man or woman madly dote
Upon the next live creature that it sees.
Fetch me this herb; and be thou here again
Ere the leviathan can swim a league.

Puck. I'll put a girdle round about the earth
In forty minutes. [*Exit* PUCK, L. 2 E.

Ober. Having once this juice,
I'll watch Titania when she is asleep,
And drop the liquor of it in her eyes:

The next thing then she waking looks upon
(Be it on lion, bear, or wolf, or bull,
Or meddling monkey, or on busy ape),
She shall pursue it with the soul of love;
And ere I take this charm off from her sight,
(As I can take it with another herb)
I'll make her render up her page to me.
[*Exit* OBERON, L.

SCENE II:—*A moon-lighted wood; a mossy bank at the back* C.; *a large tree* R.; *the whole troop of* FAIRIES *discovered in groups. Music. Enter* TITANIA *and her Train* R. U. E.

Tit. Come, now a roundel, and a fairy song;
Then, for the third part of a minute, hence:
Some, to kill cankers in the musk-rose buds;
Some, war with rear-mice for their leathern wings,
To make my small elves coats; and some keep back
The clamorous owl, that nightly hoots, and wonders
At our quaint spirits. Sing me now asleep;
Then to your offices, and let me rest.

SONG.

1st *Fairy*. *You spotted snakes, with double tongues,*
Thorny hedgehogs be not seen.
Newts and blind worms do no wrong;
Come not near our Fairy Queen.
CHORUS. *Philomel, with melody,*
Sing in our sweet lullaby;

Lulla, lulla, lullaby; lulla, lulla, lullaby:
Never harm, nor spell, nor charm,
Come our lovely lady nigh;
So, good night, with lullaby.

2d *Fairy.* *Weaving spiders, come not here;*
Hence, you long-legged spinners, hence:
Beetles black, approach not near;
Worm, nor snail, do no offense.

CHORUS. *Philomel, with melody, etc.*

1st *Fairy.* Hence, away! now all is well:
One, aloof stand sentinel.

[*Exeunt* FAIRIES, R. *and* L. TITANIA *sleeps upon the bank,* C. *Enter* OBERON, L. 2 E.

Ober. What thou seest when thou dost wake,
[*Squeezes the flower on* TITANIA'S *eyelids.*
Do it for thy true love take;
Love and languish for his sake:
Be it ounce, or cat, or bear,
Pard, or boar with bristled hair,
In thy eye that shall appear
When thou wak'st, it is thy dear.
Wake when some vile thing is near.

[*Exit* R. 3 E. *Enter* BOTTOM, *singing;* PUCK *having clapped on him an ass's head.*

SONG.

Bot. *The oosel-cock, so black of hue,*
With orange-tawny bill,
The throstle with his note so true,
The wren with little quill—

Tit. (R.) What angel wakes me from my flowery bed? [*Wakes.*

I pray thee, gentle mortal, sing again;
Mine ear is much enamored of thy note;
So is mine eye enthralled to thy shape;
And thy fair virtue's force perforce, doth move me,
On the first view, to say, to swear, I love thee.

Bot. (L.) Methinks, mistress, you should have little reason for that: and yet, to say the truth, reason and love keep little company together now-a-days. The more the pity, that some honest neighbors will not make them friends. Nay, I can gleek upon occasion.

Tit. Thou art as wise as thou art beautiful.

Bot. Not so, neither; but if I had wit enough to get out of this wood, I have enough to serve mine own turn.

Tit. Out of this wood do not desire to go:
Thou shalt remain here, whether thou wilt or no.
I am a spirit of no common rate;
The Summer still doth tend upon my state;
And I do love thee: therefore, go with me;
I'll give thee fairies to attend on thee;
And they shall fetch thee jewels from the deep,
And sing, while thou on pressed flowers dost sleep:
And I will purge thy mortal grossness so,
That thou shalt like an airy spirit go.—
Peas-blossom! Cobweb! Mote! and Mustard-seed!
[*Enter four* FAIRIES.

Peas-blossom. (R.) Ready.

Cobweb. (L.) And I.

Mote. (R.) And I.

Mustard-seed. (L.) Where shall we go?

Tit. Be kind and courteous to this gentleman:
Hop in his walks, and gambol in his eyes;
Feed him with apricots and dewberries,
With purple grapes, green figs, and mulberries.
The honey bags steal from the humblebees,
And for night tapers crop their waxen thighs,
And light them at the fiery glow-worm's eyes,
To have my love to bed and to arise;
And pluck the wings from painted butterflies,
To fan the moonbeams from his sleeping eyes;
Nod to him, elves, and do him courtesies.

[*They dance around* BOTTOM.

Peas. Hail, mortal!

Cob. Hail!

Mote. Hail!

Mus. Hail!

Bot. I cry your worship's mercy heartily.—I beseech, your worship's name.

Cob. Cobweb.

Bot. I shall desire you of more acquaintance, good Master Cobweb. If I cut my finger, I shall make bold with you.—Your name, honest gentleman?

Peas. Peas-blossom.

Bot. I pray you, commend me to Mistress Squash, your mother, and to Master Peascod, your father. Good Master Peas-blossom, I shall desire you of more acquaintance, too.—Your name, I beseech you, sir?

Mus. Mustard-seed.

Bot. Good Master Mustard-seed, I know your patience well: that same cowardly, giant-like, ox-beef hath devoured many a gentlemen of your house. I promise you, your kindred hath made my eyes water ere now. I desire you of more acquaintance, good Master Mustard-seed.

[OBERON *enters unseen* L. 2 E.

Tit. Come, sit thee down upon this flowery bed,
While I thy amiable cheeks do coy,
And stick musk-roses in thy sleek, smooth head,
And kiss thy fair large ears, my gentle joy.

Bot. Where 's Peas-blossom?

Peas. Ready.

Bot. Scratch my head, Peas-blossom.—Where 's Monsieur Cobweb?

Cob. Ready.

Bot. Monsieur Cobweb; good Monsieur, get your weapons in your hands, and kill me a red-hipped humblebee on the top of a thistle; and, good Monsieur, bring me the honey bag. Do not fret yourself too much in the action, Monsieur; and, good Monsieur, have a care the honey bag break not: I would be loath to have you overflown with a honey bag, signior.—Where 's Monsieur Mustard-seed?

Mus. Ready.

Bot. Give me your neif, Monsieur Mustard-seed. Pray you, leave your courtesy, good Monsieur.

Mus. What's your will?

Bot. Nothing, good Monsieur, but to help Cavalery Cobweb to scratch. I must to the barber's, Monsieur; for, methinks, I am marvellous hairy about the face, and I am such a tender ass, if my hair do but tickle me, I must scratch.

Tit. What, wilt thou hear some music, my sweet love?

Bot. I have a reasonable good ear in music: let 's have the tongs and the bones.

Tit. Or say, sweet love, what thou desir'st to eat.

Bot. Truly, a peck of provender: I could munch your good dry oats. Methinks, I have a great desire to a bottle of hay: good hay, sweet hay, hath no fellow.

Tit. I have a venturous fairy that shall seek
The squirrel's hoard, and fetch thee new nuts.

Bot. I had rather have a handful or two of dried peas. But, I pray you, let none of your people stir me: I have an exposition of sleep come upon me.

Tit. Sleep thou, and I will wind thee in my arms.
Fairies, be gone, and be a while away.
So doth the woodbine the sweet honeysuckle
Gently entwist; the female ivy so
Enrings the barky fingers of the elm.
Oh, how I love thee! How I dote on thee!

[*Exeunt* FAIRIES R. *and* L. *They sleep.* OBERON *advances* L. *Enter* PUCK R. 3 E. *and down* C.

Ober. Welcome, good Robin. Seest thou this sweet sight?
Her dotage now I do begin to pity;
For meeting her of late behind the wood,
Seeking sweet favors for this hateful fool,
I did upbraid her, and fall out with her.
For she his hairy temples then had rounded
With coronet of fresh and fragrant flowers;
And that same dew, which sometime on the buds
Was wont to swell like round and orient pearls,
Stood now within the pretty flow'ret's eyes,
Like tears that did their own disgrace bewail.
When I had, at my pleasure, taunted her,
And she, in mild terms, begged my patience,
I then did ask of her her changeling child,
Which straight she gave me, and her fairy sent
To bear him to my bower in Fairy-land.
And now I have the boy, I will undo
This hateful imperfection of her eyes:
And, gentle Puck, take this transformed scalp
From off the head of this Athenian swain,
That he awaking when the other do,
May all to Athens back again repair,
And think no more of this night's accidents,
But as the fierce vexation of a dream.
But first, I will release the Fairy Queen.
[*Touching her eyes with an herb.*

Be as thou wert wont to be;
See as thou wert wont to see:

Dian's bud, o'er Cupid's flower,
Hath such force and blessed power.
Now, my Titania! wake you, my sweet Queen.
Tit. My Oberon! what visions have I seen!
Methought I was enamored of an ass.
Ober. There lies your love.
Tit. How came these things to pass?
Oh, how mine eyes do loathe this visage now!
Ober. Silence a while. Robin, take off his head.
Titania, music call; and strike more dead
Than common sleep, of all these five the sense.
Tit. Music, ho! music! such as charmeth sleep.
Puck. Now, when thou wak'st, with thine own fool's eyes peep.
Ober. Sound, music! [*Still music*] Come, my Queen, take hands with me,
And rock the ground whereon these sleepers be.
Now thou and I are new in amity,
And will to-morrow midnight solemnly
Dance in Duke Theseus' house triumphantly,
And bless it to all fair posterity.
There shall the pairs of faithful lovers be
Wedded, with Theseus, all in jollity.

Puck. Fairy King, attend, and mark:
I do hear the morning lark.
Ober. Then, my Queen, in silence sad,
Trip we after the night's shade;
We the globe can compass soon,
Swifter than the wand'ring moon.

Tit. Come, my lord; and in our flight,
Tell me how it came this night,
That I sleeping here was found
With these mortals on the ground.

Curtain.

COSTUMES.

BOTTOM.—Flesh-colored arms and legs; brown shirt; ass's head.

OBERON.—Flesh-colored arms and legs; white shirt, richly spangled; blue gauze drapery spangled; jeweled head-dress, and belt; rich sandals.

TITANIA.—Blue gauze dress, with silver-spangled trimming; blue gauze robe, spangled; jeweled coronet; sandals.

PUCK.—White muslin shirt, trimmed with silver; flesh-colored arms and legs; silvered sandals; silver-flowered head-dress; gauze and silver wings.

FAIRIES.—White muslin dresses, with gauze draperies, trimmed with silver spangles; wings; wands.

REMARKS AND SUGGESTIONS.

For the title and arrangement of this little play, the editor is indebted to *Leigh Hunt's Selections from the English Poets.* Nothing can exceed the poetic beauty of the fairy speeches, particularly those of Oberon and Titania. They should be studied with critical attention, and rendered in a manner worthy of their wonderful grace and sweetness. To mar such language in the delivery is a high crime against Poesie.

The instrumental accompaniments required in the play may be selected from Mendelssohn's celebrated music to *A Midsummer Night's Dream.* The vocal music of Shakespeare's plays, with piano-forte accompaniment, is published by Samuel French, 122 Nassau Street, New York.

In painting the forest scene, the artist would do well to put in a good deal of foliage, bushes, etc. The ass's head can be bought or hired in any city, at the masquerade stores, or at the theaters. The characters on the stage, at the close of the last scene, should take such positions as to form a picturesque group, which may be illuminated just before the curtain falls.

MRS. WILLIS'S WILL.

A Comic Drama.

From Lacy's Home Plays for Ladies.

PERSONS REPRESENTED.

MRS. ROBINSON, *aged forty, Mrs. Willis's executrix.*
LADY SPINDLE, *aged forty, absurdly haughty and dignified.*
MRS. DWINDLE, *aged thirty, a poetess and lady of fashion.*
JENNY, *aged eighteen, a farm servant.*
RACHEL, *aged fifty, Mrs. Robinson's servant.*

SCENE:—*The general chamber of an old farm-house, plainly but comfortably furnished; door of entrance,* C.; *doors,* L. 2 E. *and* L. 1 E.; *door,* R. 1 E.; L. C., *against the scene, a writing table; a table,* R. C., *with a desk on it; a bureau,* R., *on which is a large looking-glass; arm chairs, easy chairs, etc.;* MRS. ROBINSON *at writing table;* RACHEL *closing the bureau drawers.*

Mrs. R. And those are the last, Rachel?

Rachel. Yes, ma'am, the inventory of all the poor, dear, dead lady's property is now complete, and the heirs may come as soon as they please.

Mrs. R. [*Rising*] As testamentary executrix, I have written to them, and believe they will be here this very day.

Rachel. While poor Mrs. Willis was alive nobody came near her, and you would have supposed that she had not a relation in the world: but no sooner is she dead, than they spring up like mushrooms.

Mrs. R. Easily accounted for. She was of humble origin, and her relatives, while she lived, were ashamed of her; but they are not too proud to inherit her property. The connections of Mr. Willis were always of opinion that he had degraded himself and them by marrying a mere peasant.

Rachel. It was just the case with my poor, dead husband, who was a drum-major in the 99th. But are these relatives of Mr. Willis such very great people?

Mrs. R. [L. *Smiling*] You will be able to judge for yourself presently. In the first place, there is Lady Spindle.

Rachel. Oh, I know! she has a fine mansion in London, and a rickety old house in the country somewhere.

Mrs. R. And gained her title through her marriage with a rickety old lord. Then there is Mrs. Dwindle, a London fine lady, who sports an abundance of crinoline, and writes nonsensical verses.

Rachel. That 's just like the man that played the trombone in the 99th—the verses, I mean, not the crinoline.

Mrs. R. [*Laughing*] Always some reminiscence of your husband's regiment—but I have a few matters to attend to. Make haste, Rachel, and finish putting the room in order. [*Exit, door* L. 2 E.

Rachel. [*Arranging and dusting chairs, etc.*] Ah, she is a good creature; the best woman I have ever known, except my poor Peter—no I don't mean that: poor Peter was n't a woman, but he was the best—

[JENNY *appears, at door* C., *and remains timidly.*

Jenny. If you please, misses, does n't my godmother live here?

Rachel. Your godmother, child! how should I know anything about your godmother?

Jenny. She was once a drum-major.

Rachel. What? You mean she married a drum-major.

Jenny. Very likely.

Rachel. Rachel Blustrus?

Jenny. Yes, that 's her.

Rachel. Oh, then it 's me you are looking for.

Jenny. [*Coming forward*] You—you are Mrs. Blustrus?

Rachel. Yes, but surely you can't be—

Jenny. Yes, I am; I 'm Jenny Roberts, the daughter of Martha Roberts, who was the wife of Thomas Roberts.

Rachel. My goddaughter?

Jenny. Yes, that I really am—will you let me kiss you, godmother? I have washed my face.

Rachel. Come along, then, poor little pussy. [*Embracing and kissing her*] Why, [*looking at her*] it 's scarcely credible; surely you can't be so tall as this?

Jenny. No, I am not quite; because I have got such thick high-lows on.

Rachel. Well, I should never have recognized you.

Jenny. And I did n't know you, a morsel; but I suppose that 's because I never saw you before.

Rachel. And I have not seen you since you were quite a tiny baby. But how comes it you are here at Churnley?

Jenny. Because I have been living about a mile away.

Rachel. With whom?

Jenny. With Farmer Stubbins—he hired me to milk the cows, and feed the pigs, and look after the poultry, and such like odd jobs—and I had plenty of hard work to do, I can tell you; but one of the little pigs rolled into the trough, and, after eating as much as he could, laid down in it and was smothered—so Farmer Stubbins stopped my wages, and bundled me off without a moment's notice.

Rachel. Poor child! So you are now without a situation?

Jenny. Yes, godmother. And having by good luck heard of you, I have come to ask you to get me a place—I do n't care what sort of place it is, I 'm not above any kind of honest work. If I had a good missus, I 'd be as faithful to her as I was to the pigs.

Rachel. [*Laughing*] In that case she would be smothered. But what can you do: do you know how to make yourself useful in a kitchen?

Jenny. I should think I did! Why I used to make all the mashes for the pigs, and roll up all the boluses for the turkeys.

Rachel. I mean, can you do the household work?

Jenny. Yes, I know—why, when any of the chickens was n't right, I always knew how to cure them.

Rachel. Well, we must see what can be done for you. I suppose you have some recommendation from somebody—some written paper which testifies to your good conduct?

Jenny. Mr. Ruler, the schoolmaster, is preparing one for me—and is going to set forth how I am an orphan, who were my parents, and all about me. He was to give it to me this morning, when he came to market—he 's in the village by this time, I dare say.

Rachel. Run to him, then, and when you return I 'll show you to Mrs. Robinson.

Jenny, Oh, thank 'ee, godmother; I have always told every body that I was certain if I could find you, you would be a friend to me.

Rachel. I 'll do the best I can for you, poor thing.

Jenny. (R.) I may leave my bundle here, may n't I?

Rachel. (L.) What bundle?

Jenny. [*Pointing to small bundle which she has left on chair, near door*] Here it is! two petticoats, and a pair of stockings—I sha'n't be long, godmother. [*Stopping at door*] Oh, dear, here 's a grand carriage stopping.

Rachel. A carriage?

Jenny. And two such beautiful ladies getting out.

Rachel. [*At door, looking off*] Oh, goodness—these are the inheritors of Mrs. Willis's property.

Jenny. Oh, godmother, look at that fine lady—she waddles just like the lame old turkey I had to look after.

Rachel. [*Lowering her voice*] Hold your tongue, you little goose.

Jenny. And look at the other staring about her through a little bit of glass. [*Imitates eye-glass*] Has she got only one eye, I wonder?

Rachel. Will you be quiet?

[*Enter* LADY SPINDLE *and* MRS. DWINDLE, *at door*, C.

Lady S. (R. C.) No one to receive us—what insolent neglect!

Mrs. D. [R. *looking through glass*] What a miserable hole.

Rachel. [*Advancing* L. C.] I beg pardon, ladies; but—

Lady S. Oh, at last, here 's some one!

Mrs. D. [*Using glass*] Who are you—the charwoman?

Rachel. Certainly not, I am assistant housekeeper, and widow of the sergeant-major of the 99th.

Lady S. [R. C., *disdainfully*] A sergeant-major—

Mrs. D. [R., *retreating*] Horrible!

Jenny. [L., *aside*] A sergeant-major do n't seem to agree with them.

Lady S. [*Pointing*] Who is that young girl?

Rachel. My goddaughter, ma'am.

Jenny. [*Curtseying*] Jenny Roberts, mum, happy to serve you, mum, I 've been used to look after pigs, and—

Mrs. D. What does she say? pigs? horrible! You hear, Lady Spindle—there are actually people of the lower orders, who have the care of pigs.

Jenny. If they was n't taken care of, your ladyships would n't never have any pork.

Lady S. } Pork!
Mrs. D. } Horrible!

Jenny. Horrible? Now, *I* think it 's beautiful, when there 's plenty of sage and onions, and nice brown crackling.

Lady S. [*Sternly*] Silence, girl!

Rachel. [*Tittering*] Hush, child!

Lady S. Inform Mrs. Robinson that I am here—I, formerly Miss Jingle—

Jenny. [*Aside*] I wonder anybody could be found to change her name for her!

Lady S. Now Lady Spindle. Say, too, that Mrs. Dwindle has also arrived.

Mrs. D. From London.

Lady S. Why do you not go, woman? How dare you keep us waiting?

Rachel. [*Aside, as she goes off* L.] What airs!

Jenny. [*Following*] What a stuck up couple!

Lady S. These persons are too ignorant to appreciate us.

Mrs. D. In the country, all the people are savages.

[*Arranging her dress, and admiring herself in the glass*, R.

Lady S. I know not how I was able to persuade myself to quit my town mansion for this miserable inheritance.

Mrs. D. [*Still admiring herself*] I shall be sadly missed from the ranks of fashion.

Lady S. And I have been compelled to renounce becoming sponsor to a new bell at our church.

Mrs. D. And I was about to read my last new elegy, "On a Dying Tittlebat," to our celebrated literary society. [*Reciting pompously*] "See how it gasps—See how it twists—See how it wriggles—See how it kicks—See—"

Lady S. I should have been received with all the honors that were formerly rendered to my noble ancestors.

Mrs. D. A tremendous ovation was prepared for me.

Lady S. And to abandon all this for Mrs. Willis's will—a mere peasant.

Mrs. D. With no poetry in her soul.

Lady S. Who made herself one of our family against our inclination.

Mrs. D. [*Admiring herself*] And who never knew how to dress in her life.

Lady S. [*Speaking lower, and with eagerness*] Have you any idea what fortune she has left?

Mrs. D. [*Ditto*] I have been assured that she was very comfortably off.

Lady S. [*As before*] 'T is probable—her early poverty had taught her to economise.

Mrs. D. [*As before*] For the benefit of her heirs.

Lady S. [*Resuming her lofty tone*] But, really, I blush that I should be compelled to stoop thus to the succession of a parvenu—I, Lady Spindle, descended, on my late husband's side, from most illustrious ancestry.

Mrs. D. [*Also resuming her former manner*] And would anybody believe that Mrs. Dwindle, who guides the fashionable world of London, and who has written so many unpublished verses—would anybody, I say, believe that the accomplished authoress of the beautiful elegy "On a Dying Tittlebat" could so far forget her dignity for a paltry share of probably a very paltry inheritance?

Lady S. After all, we owe something to our relations.

Mrs. D. Certainly, if they *will* leave property behind them, it would not look well should we refuse to accept it! [*In a lower tone, and quickly to* LADY S.] I hope she has not had the audacity to bequeath her fortune to any other than us.

Lady S. Oh, what an idea! her memory would be dishonored for ever.

Mrs. D. In fact, we have always reckoned upon her money.

Lady S. Consequently, it belongs to us of right!

Mrs. D. That is quite clear. [*Amiably*] I see, your ladyship, that we admirably understand each other.

Lady S. Nothing more simple, with people of quality; but, if I am not mistaken, here is the testamentary executrix. [*Enter* MRS. ROBINSON, L. 2 E.

Mrs. R. A thousand pardons for not having sooner waited on you. I was searching for the copy of my dear friend's will—that testament which I am charged to make known to you.

Lady S. 'T is well, madam; we will allow you to make the communication. [*Sits.*

Mrs. D. Above all, avoid details, I beg of you, and come at once to the essential point—that is to say, the amount of the sum we are to receive. [*Sits.*

Lady S. Precisely! Do n't be prosy!

Mrs. D. No, do n't! I hate prose!

Mrs. R. [*Looking at them*] Umph! Pray be seated, ladies.

Lady S. [*Haughtily*] Proceed!

Mrs. D. [*Looking through eye-glass*] We are listening, my good woman.

Mrs. R. I am too polite, ladies, to allow myself to stand. [*Sinking into easy chair.*

Lady S. [*Aside,* R.] What does she mean by that?

Mrs. D. [*Aside,* R. C.] What vulgar impertinence.

Mrs. R. (L.) You are no doubt aware that a short

time before her death, my dear friend, Mrs. Willis, paid a visit to the village in which she was born, and which, to the last, she passionately loved.

Lady S. What a plebeian idea! [*To* MRS. ROBINSON] And where is this village situated?

Mrs. R. In the center of Cheshire.

Mrs. D. Horrible! [*Turning up her nose*] Why, that is the place where they manufacture all the cheeses.

Mrs. R. It was always a pleasing recollection to my poor friend that, in her early days, she had helped to manufacture many a cheese; but her journey thither had a more important object than making or tasting cheese. She wished to ascertain if any members of her own family were still surviving.

Lady S. In order that she might favor them at our expense—shameful!

Mrs. D. For them she would have robbed us of our just rights—unnatural woman!

Lady S. When a person has the honor to possess such relations as we, she should know better than to search for others.

Mrs. R. Reassure yourselves—Mrs. Willis could discover none of her own family, and it was then that she resolved on making the will, which gives to you her whole fortune.

Lady S. Read the document!

Mrs. D. Make haste, my good woman!

Mrs. R. You must know, ladies, in the first place,

that the fortune Mrs. Willis has left consists of two very extensive farms, worth, each of them, about four thousand pounds.

Mrs. D.
Lady S. } Four thousand pounds!

Mrs. D. Poor, dear Mrs. Willis!

Lady S. I have always felt assured she was a most estimable woman.

Mrs. R. She possessed, besides, a forest, of the estimated value of three thousand five hundred pounds.

Lady S.
Mrs. D. } A forest!

Mrs. R. With a mill and some meadows, which produced her a yearly rental of about a hundred pounds.

Mrs. D. Why, altogether, it forms a fortune.

Lady S. The poor, dear, kind, old lady!

Mrs. D. I am quite affected!

Lady S. Where is my dear, dear cousin Mrs. Willis's will?

Mrs. R. [*Showing it, and smiling*] Here it is! I will pass immediately to that part of it in which you are interested.

[*The two* LADIES *bend eagerly toward* MRS. ROBINSON.

Lady S.
Mrs. D. } Yes, do, do!

Mrs. R. [*Reading*] "I, the widow of—, etc., having been unable to discover any of my own relations, whom I would gladly have enriched, have, therefore, decided to bequeath my fortune to the relatives of my husband."

Mrs. D. Worthy woman!

Lady S. She was an honor to her sex!

Mrs. R. [*Reading*] "Those relatives are reduced to two; the first, Lady Spindle, who, in striving always to appear noble, simply proves that she is perfectly ridiculous."

Lady S. [*Who has been listening with a smiling air*] What's that?

Mrs. D. [*Laughing*] Oh, nothing—a mere jest, through a very good one—ha, ha, ha! our dear cousin was so full of wit. [*To* MRS. R.] Pray go on.

Mrs. R. [*Reading*] "The next is Mrs. Dwindle, a London would-be fine lady, and a self-styled poet, whose verses are as weak as herself."

Mrs. D. What's that?

Lady S. [*Laughing*] Nothing. Our dear cousin is only repeating what, no doubt, she has often heard; and she was, you know, so full of wit. [*To* MRS. R.] Pray go on.

Mrs. R. [*Reading*] "In default of relatives of my own, those two ladies will share my succession between them."

Lady S.
Mrs. E. } Good creature!

Mrs. R. "But not unless they shall comply with the following conditions:—"

Lady S.
Mrs. D. } Conditions! Are there conditions?

Mrs. R. [*Reading*] "As I have no wish to enrich persons who would despise the state from which I rose, I exact that these ladies shall not be suffered to share in my fortune until after they shall, both of them, have dressed themselves in a peasant's habit, precisely similar to that which I formerly wore."

Lady S.
Mrs. D. } [*Starting up*] Ah!

Mrs. R. [*Continuing, with great emphasis*] "And not until they shall have shown themselves in that costume to Mrs. Robinson, my testamentary executrix, and shall have danced a country jig in her presence."

Lady S.
Mrs. D. } What atrocity!

Lady S. I dance a country jig!

Mrs. D. I dress as a common peasant!

Lady S. Absurd!

Mrs. D. Horrible!

Lady S. Your friend, madam, was an impertinent woman.

Mrs. D. We will not comply with such conditions.

Mrs. R. [*Rising*] Then you renounce the inheritance?

Lady S. Eh?

Mrs. D. Ah!

Mrs. R. [*Smiling*] Take time to reflect, ladies. Meanwhile, this house, which belonged to Mrs. Willis, is entirely at your disposal. That way an apartment has been prepared for your ladyship.

[*Pointing to room*, L. 1 E.] Your chamber, madam [*To* MRS. DWINDLE], is yonder. [*Pointing to door*, R.] Should you need anything, have the kindness to ring, and Rachel will obey your orders. [*Going up, and returning*] You will, ladies, each of you, find in your apartment a complete dress, resembling, in every particular, that which was worn by my poor friend when, an humble peasant girl in her native village, she was employed in making cheese.

Mrs. D. [*Turning away indignantly*] Cheese—pah!

Lady S. [*Ditto*] Oh, this is too much!

[MRS. ROBINSON *salutes them and goes off*, L. 2 E.

Lady S. What insolence.

Mrs. D. If I were in London, I should have a nervous attack.

Lady S. These common people actually believe that we care for their wealth.

Mrs. D. We are quite above that, I should hope, while the world of fashion and of literature are left to us.

Lady S. If I regret anything of the inheritance, it is only the farms, because farming is now a fashionable pursuit.

Mrs. D. I chiefly regret the forest, because trees and birds, with the hares and rabbits, and the hedgehogs, are so poetical.

Lady S. And then the mill.—I should certainly like to have a mill.

Mrs. D. And then the meadows—full of buttercups and daisies, and beautiful butterflies—how delightful to watch the grass grow—

Lady S. And then to sell the hay.

Mrs. D. [*Sentimentally*] Oh, your ladyship feels, as I do, all the charms of nature. But these treasures are offered to us at an impossible price.

Lady S. To accept them would for ever degrade us in society.

Mrs. D. So that we are decided, are we not?

Lady S. Perfectly decided!

Mrs. D. You promise that you will not fulfill the the obnoxious clauses of the will?

Lady S. Certainly! And you?

Mrs. D. Positively!

Lady S. Believe me, I have ceased to think of the matter.

Mrs. D. I assure you I have quite forgotten all about it.

Lady S. [*Aside*] Such wealth! how it would elevate the noble name of Spindle.

Mrs. D. [*Aside*] Such a fortune! what importance it would give to the fashionable name of Dwindle! [*Enter* RACHEL *and* JENNY, L.

Rachel. Those, then, are the papers you were promised?

Jenny. [*Papers in her hand*] Yes, godmother, and Mr. Ruler says they are all correct and explanationary, I think he called it.

Rachel. Well, sit down, and I will go to Mrs. Robinson. [*Goes off*, L. 2 E.

Lady S. Oh, here is the little pig girl again.

Mrs. D. And this is the dress they wish us to wear. [*Both ladies walk round* JENNY.

Jenny. [*Aside*] These are the heiresses—how they are looking me over. [*She curtseys.*

Lady S. [*Aside*] I am glad to have an opportunity of observing how these clownish habits are worn. [*Puts on spectacles.*

Mrs. D. [R. *looking at* JENNY *through eye-glass*] I must see how the cap is stuck on.

Jenny. [*Aside, confused*] Whatever are they staring at—has somebody pinned something on my back, I wonder? [*Looking herself over.*

Lady S. [*Aside*] After all, a lady of quality would give some dignity to that humble costume.

Mrs. D. [*Aside*] The dress is not so very unbecoming—the petticoat is short, but when one has a well-turned ankle—

Jenny. [*Aside, more and more confused*] There is certainly something the matter with me. [*Aloud*] Hem! hem! [*Aside*] It can't be manners to stare like that, as if a body was a peep-show. [*Coughing loudly*] Hem! hem!

[*Turns her back on* LADY SPINDLE *and* MRS. DWINDLE, *and goes up, singing.*

Mrs. D. [*Aside, quickly*] Ah, to be sure; if only one of us should obey the conditons imposed, that one would have all.

Lady S. [*Aside, in deep thought*] If I only disguise myself, I alone shall inherit.

Mrs. D. [*Aside, having formed a resolution*] It shall be so! [*Aloud to* LADY SPINDLE] Lady Spindle, nothing now detains me here, and I shall instantly depart for London.

Lady S. And I for my country mansion.

Mrs. D. I have your word?

Lady S. And I yours?

Mrs. D. [*Saluting*] Lady Spindle!

Lady S. [*Saluting grandly*] Madam—

[MRS. DWINDLE *goes toward back, as if about to leave, then, as* LADY SPINDLE *turns away, she darts off* R. E.

Lady S. [*Looking round, and not seeing her*] She is gone—now then! [*Darts off* L. 1 E.

Jenny. [*Who has observed them*] Why, whatever is the matter with them—they darted into the rooms as if they were going to steal something. I wonder where they went to school? How they did stare at me. I felt as if I should like to hide myself in my pockets. [*Enter* RACHEL, L. 2 E.

Rachel. I can't find— [*Enter* MRS. ROBINSON, L. 2 E.] Oh, here you are, ma'am! Jenny, this is Mrs. Robinson. [*Pushes* JENNY *to* MRS. R., L.

Jenny. [*Bobbing a curtsey*] Servant, ma'am!

Mrs. R. So, my child, you want a situation?

Jenny. [*Timidly*] Yes, ma'am.

Rachel. (R.) Do n't be frightened, missus won't eat you. [*To* MRS. ROBINSON] She 's just like I was before I married the drum-major of the 99th. [*To* JENNY] Speak up and say what you want.

[RACHEL *arranges some of the things at back, and bustles off*, L. 2 E.

Jenny. If you please, ma'am [*growing bolder*], I should like to take care of your pigs, and look after the poultry, or nurse your children, or anybody else's, or do any sort of work that would earn my bread, with a little bit of butter on it.

Mrs. R. [*Smiling*] That is to say, you want a comfortable situation?

Jenny. I am not particular for myself; but I have a little brother, he is too young to do anything for himself yet, and so, you know, ma'am, as I 'm his sister, I 'm in duty bound to do for him—bless his pretty little heart!

Mrs. R. Ah, Rachel told me nothing of that.

Jenny. [*Lowering her voice*] Because I told her nothing about it. I did n't wish to be too much of a bother to godmother the first time I saw her. If I had told her about Peter, she might perhaps have thought that I was asking for charity—and I did n't come here for that. As long as I can work, Peter shall need nothing from anybody, except their friendship. I am his elder sister, and he is my child, now poor mother is dead, and little Peter shall find me as good as a mother to him.

Mrs. D. [*Interested*] You are a worthy girl, Jenny.

Jenny. [*Curtseying*] Am I, ma'am?

Mrs. R. Then you have no relation living.

Jenny. Yes, I have, ma'am—I 've got Peter.

Mrs. R. Is he in this village?

Jenny. Along with Mrs. Britain, who treats him like a prince; and no wonder, for he 's a beauty—especially now that he has got my best petticoat made into a new dress—and he is as proud as a peacock, and so loving, and so obedient—never have to speak to him twice, the little dear! He 's a perfect angel—only I can't make him keep his nose clean.

Mrs. R. And you two are all that are left of your family?

Jenny. [*Sadly*] Ah, yes!

Mrs. R. Did your parents live in this village?

Jenny. No, ma'am! My parents, as I have heard say, were born a good way off from here, in a village called Frierly.

Mrs. R. In Derbyshire!

Jenny. Yes, ma'am.

Mrs. R. And what was your father's name?

Jenny. Roberts, ma'am, Thomas Roberts—and my mother's name was—

Mrs. R. Roberts! Surely that is the name which—Have you no documents that might—

Jenny. No, ma'am, I have n't got any documents, but here are some papers, which Mr. Ruler, the schoolmaster, gave me; they are my character and my birth and parentage, and they tell all about me and little brother Peter.

[*Pointing to papers which she has left on the writing-table*, L. C.

Mrs. R. Let me see them.

[*Goes to writing-table and commences examining* JENNY'S *papers.* RACHEL *re-enters* L. 2 E. *and goes to* JENNY.

Rachel. Did I not tell you there was no occasion to be afraid—nobody has any business to be afraid, as my husband used to say, when he was drum-major of the 99th. [*Arranges things.*

Jenny. [*Alone in front*] Well, certainly that lady does seem a very nice woman.

Mrs. R. Oh, Heaven! is it possible?

Jenny. [*Jumping round hastily*] Oh, gracious! what is it?

Rachel. [*Turning toward* MRS. ROBINSON, R.] A spider, perhaps.

Mrs. R. Ah, my dear child, if it were really true! Little Peter and yourself would never need again to ask for aught.

Jenny.
Rachel. } Eh?

Mrs. R. A moment! I must be very certain before I speak.

[*Unlocks desk,* R. C., *and examines papers.*

Rachel. [*Aside to* JENNY] She will get you a good place, you'll see. [*Goes toward* MRS. R.

Jenny. Perhaps I shall have to look after the pigs and poultry in some great lord's house. Oh, that would be nice; and little Peter should come and see me; and I would show him how I am getting up in the world. Oh, the very thought of it makes me feel as if I could jump over the moon.

[LADY SPINDLE *enters door*, L. 1 E., *and advances without seeing the others, who are at back.*

Lady S. [*Aside*] Mrs Dwindle is gone, and I am sole heiress.

Jenny. [*Seeing her*] Hey! here is some other girl come to look after a place.

[*Enter* MRS. DWINDLE, R. E.

Mrs. D. [*Aside*] Now, then, the entire fortune will fall to me!

Jenny. [*Aside*] And there's another! Does everybody come here to look after poultry and pigs?

[MRS. ROBINSON *is up stage*, R. C., *her back toward audience, and showing papers to* RACHEL, *who exhibits great astonishment;* JENNY *is also toward back of stage*, L. C., *so that the front of stage is left to the two* LADIES, *who advance, not seeing each other till they meet*, C., *when both start back in great amazement.*

Mrs. D. What do I see?

Lady S. What do I behold?

Mrs. D. Oh, what perfidy!

Lady S. Oh, what treachery!

Rachel.
Mrs. R. } [*Turning toward* LADIES] Ah!

Mrs. R. [*Laughing*] I was sure of it!

Rachel. Who are these two queer animals?

Mrs. D. Is this the way you keep your promise, madam?

Lady S. This proves how well your word may be depended on!

Mrs. D. You hoped to exclude me from the inheritance!

Lady S. You wished to rob me!

Mrs. D. I am fulfilling the conditions of the will, madam!

Lady S. And so am I, madam!

Mrs. D. I have a straw bonnet and short petticoat!

Lady S. And I have a pair of high-lows!

Mrs. D. And I shall dance a country jig!

Lady S. And so shall I, madam!

Mrs. D. Not before me, madam!

[*Both commence dancing ridiculously, both at same time singing a country jig;* RACHEL *and* JENNY *shout with laughter;* MRS. ROBINSON *laughs more moderately; after a while all three advance.*

Mrs. R. Enough, ladies, enough!

Lady S. You are a witness, madam, that I have obeyed Mrs. Willis's Will.

Mrs. D. So have I.

Lady S. The inheritance belongs to me.

Mrs. D. Of course I shall have my portion.

Jenny. And have they been jumping about like that for money? [*To them*] You would get ever so much at our fair next week.

Lady S. } *Mrs. D.* } Insolent!

Mrs. R. You have certainly, ladies, earned the right to inherit, *if there was no living relative of my poor friend's;* but, while thanking you for the delightful exhibition you have just afforded us [*taking* JENNY'S *hand*], I here beg leave to present to you the true and only heiress!

Jenny. I!

Lady S. }
Mrs. D. } She!

Rachel. Jenny!

Mrs. R. By the merest accident I have just discovered in this young girl, a niece of Mrs. Willis's.

Rachel. }
Jenny. } Ah!

Lady S. }
Mrs. D. } Oh!

Mrs. R. Consequently, that clause in the testament is of no effect, and it is to Jenny that all belongs.

Jenny. Oh, can it be?

Lady S. My legs sink under me!

[*Falling into arm chair,* L.

Mrs. D. I am annihilated!

[*Falling into arm chair,* R.

Rachel. It's wonderful! but just such another case happened when my poor husband was drum-major of the 99th.

Jenny. All to me! oh, godmother! oh, Mrs. Robinson! Why, then, I am rich—rich! Oh, what happiness for little brother Peter—what splendid dresses he shall have—and such a beautiful dinner every day—and every night, just before he goes to bed, such a nice hot supper. And I'll give such a lot of money to all the poor people—and nobody, not even the poultry and the pigs—except these two ladies, shall have cause to regret that to poor orphan Jenny and her little brother Peter has fallen all the property left by Mrs. Willis's Will.

Mrs. D. seated R. *Lady S. seated* L.
Mrs. R. Jenny. Rachel.

COSTUMES.

LADY SPINDLE. — Extravagantly fashionable dress. Second dress: Blue short petticoat, thick half boots, white cotton jacket, with short sleeves, large cotton cap, and straw bonnet.

MRS. DWINDLE.—Extravagantly fashionable dress; eye glass. Second dress: Same as Lady Spindle's second dress.

MRS. ROBINSON.—Mourning suit.

RACHEL.—Plain black merino dress, cap, and black ribbon.

JENNY.—Brown merino frock, little grey cloak, straw bonnet, grey stockings, half boots.

LITTLE RED RIDING-HOOD.

Drama and Pantomime.

By Tom Hood.

PERSONS REPRESENTED.

JACK, *a wood-cutter; afterward* HARLEQUIN.

THE WOLF, *afterward* CLOWN.

DAME MARGERY, *mother of Little Red Riding-hood; afterward* PANTALOON.

LITTLE RED RIDING-HOOD, *afterward* COLUMBINE.

THE FAIRY FELICIA.

BUTCHERS, BAKERS, SWEEPS, *tag-rag and bob-tail generally, for the comic business.*

SCENE I:—*The exterior of* LITTLE RED RIDING-HOOD'S *cottage. Enter her* MOTHER. *She runs about the stage, looking for her child.*

Mother. Red Riding-hood! Red Riding-hood, I say!
Where can the little monkey hide away?
Red Riding-hood! Oh, deary, deary me!
Provoking child, where-ever can she be?
[*Looks off on both sides.*
She is a shocking disobedient child,
Enough to drive a loving mother wild;
But stay! where are the butter and the cake
That to her grandmother she has to take?
[*Fetches basket from cottage, and shows cake and butter.*
Here is the cake, and here 's the butter, see!
The nicest cake and butter that could be.
These in this basket I will neatly lay,
A present to poor granny to convey.
They are not tithes, though given to the wicker;
[*Puts them in basket.*
Bless me, I wish the child were only quicker!
Red Riding-hood, Red Riding-hood! Dear, dear!
[*Enter* LITTLE RED RIDING-HOOD.
R. R. H. Here I am, ma.
Mother. You wicked puss, come here!
Take this to granny! Poor old soul, she 's ill;
Give her my love, and these tid-bits.
R. R. H. I will.
Won't it be nice? Through wood and field I 'll walk,

And have with Jack, perhaps, a little talk.
Dear Jack! At thought of him why quickly beat, heart?
Dear Jack! he's no Jack-pudding, but a sweet-tart!
Won't I catch butterflies and gather flowers!

Mother. Mind you don't dwadle and be gone for hours,
But go straight there, and back again with speed,
And do not loiter in lane, wood, or mead;
Or else a great big wolf shall come to eat you.
At any rate, your loving mother 'll beat you!

[*Threatens* R. R. H. *with stick. Enter* JACK *at back.*

Jack. Where is Red Riding-hood, my heart's delight?
La, there's her mother! What a horrid fright!

Mother. What are you doing here, you rascal Jack?
Be off, or I will hit you in a crack.

[*Strikes at him, but misses.*

Jack. Before your hits, ma'am, I prefer a miss;

[*Bows to* R. R. H.

So blow for blow, I mean to blow a kiss.

[*Kisses hand to* R. R. H.

Mother. Kisses be blo——.

Jack. Hush! don't be coarse and low:
If you don't like my company, I'll go;
Your words are violent, your temper quick,
So this young wood-cutter will cut his stick.

[*He and* R. R. H. *exchange signs, blow kisses, etc. Exit* JACK.

Mother. [*To* R. R. H.] That spark is not your match, you 're to blame,
To take delight in such a paltry flame.
Now go; and lose no time upon the road,
But hasten straight to grandmother's abode.
R. R. H. I will not loiter, mother, by the way,
Nor go in search of butterflies astray.
Instead of picking flowers, my steps I 'll pick,
And take the things to granny, who is sick.
Good-bye, dear mother.
Mother. [*Kisses her*] There, my dear, good-bye.
R. R. H. See how obedient to your word I fly!
Mother. A one-horse fly! What nonsense you do talk!
You have no wings, and so of course must walk.
You go afoot. How now, miss? Wherefore smile?
R. R. H Why go a foot? I 've got to go a mile;
That was the reason, mother, why I smiled.
Mother. That joke 's so far-fetched, that it 's very miled. [*Exeunt.*

SCENE II:—*A Forest Glade. Enter* RED RIDING-HOOD.

R. R. H. How nice the wood is, with its cool green shade!
I must sit down and rest here, I 'm afraid;
Though mother would declare I 'm only lazy,
I 'm very tired and weary. [*Yawns, then sees flower and starts*] Lawk! a daisy! [*Picks it.*
It can't be wrong some pretty flowers to pull;

With them I 'll fill my little apron full,
And take to please my poor old granny's eye.
[*Butterfly flies across stage.*
Oh, is n't that a lovely butterfly! [*Runs after it.*
Stop, little butterfly, a moment, do.
[*Tries to catch it, and runs into the arms of* JACK, *who enters.*
I 've caught it.

Jack. Beg your pardon, I 've caught you. [*Kisses her.*

R. R. H. Do n't you be rude, sir! Fie, why treat me thus?

Jack. You thought to take a fly, I took a bus.
I love you, pretty maid. Suppose we say
That we 'll be married? Just you fix the day. [*Embraces her.*

R. R. H. You 're very pressing, sir! Well, let me see;
Next Wednesday a wedding's day shall be.

Jack. An earlier date far better, dear, will do;
Say, why not Toosday as the day for two?
Another kiss!

R. R. H. A kiss? Oh, dear me, no!
Farewell. To poor old granny's I must go,
For mother has commanded me to take
The poor old soul some butter and a cake.

Jack I 'm off to work, then.

R. R. H. Whither go you, pray?

Jack. I 'm not quite sure, but mean to ax my way. [*Exit.*

R. R. H. Now I must hurry off to granny.

[FAIRY *appears.*

La!

How lovely! such a sight I never saw.

Fairy. I am a fairy, and your friend, my dear;
You 'll need my aid, for there is danger near.
Your disobedience to your mother's will
Has given bad fairies power to work you ill.

R. R. H. Thanks, beauteous fairy. But no harm I meant,
And of my disobedience much repent.

Fairy. I know it, and will therefore prove your friend;
You shall o'ercome your troubles in the end.
Remember when your case my help demands,
You 've naught to do save simply clap your hands.

[*Exit* FAIRY.

R. R. H. How very sorry I am now, that I
Was disobedient, let the time slip by;
Neglected granny and my mother's words,
To gather flowers and list to singing birds;
To hunt the butterflies 't was wrong, I fear—
But, goodness gracious me, what have we here?

[*Enter* WOLF.

Wolf. Oh, what a very pretty little girl!
Such rosy cheeks, such hair, so nice in curl!
[*Aside*] As tender as a chicken, too, I 'll lay;
One does n't get such tid-bits every day.

[*To* R. R. H.

What brings you wandering in the wood like this,

And whither are you going, pretty miss?

R. R. H. I'm bound to granny's cottage, but I fear
I've strayed from the right path in coming here.
I'm taking her a currant-cake and butter;
So nice, their excellence no tongue can utter.

Wolf. [*Aside*] However excellent, I'll bet I lick it;
As to the cake, I'll gobble pretty quick it.
[*To* R. R. H.] And where does granny live?

R. R. H. Not far from this:
It's near the river.

Wolf. [*Pointing off*] Then, my little miss,
Along that path you have but to repair,
And very shortly you will find you're there.

R. R. H. Oh, thank you; now I'll go.

[*Exit singing.*

Wolf. And I'll be bound
You'll find that same short cut a long way round.
The nearest road I'll to the cottage take,
And of old granny I short work will make,
And then I'll gobble you up, little dear.
I didn't like to try and eat you here;
You might object to it—some people do—
And scream, and cry, and make a hubbubboo;
And there's a wood-cutter, I know, hard by,
From whose quick hatchet quick-catch-it should I.
Here goes to bolt old granny without flummery,
A spring—and then one swallow shall be summery!

[*Exit.*

SCENE III:—*Interior of* GRANDMOTHER'S *cottage. On the right hand, close to the wing, a bed containing a dummy with a large night-cap.* WOLF *is heard knocking.*

Granny. [*Spoken from the wing close by the bed.* Who 's there?

Wolf. [*Imitating* R. R. H.] Your little grandchild, granny dear.

Granny. That child has got a shocking cold, that's clear.
Some carelessness—she 's got her feet wet through
With running in the rain or heavy dew,
Perhaps without her bonnet; and of course,
The little donkey is a little hoarse,
Her words she used not croakingly to utter.—
What do you want?

Wolf. I 've brought your cake and butter,
But can't come in, the door my strength defies.

Granny. Pull at the bobbin, and the latch will rise. [*Enter* WOLF.

Granny. How are you, little darling?

Wolf. Darling! Pooh!
You did n't bolt your door, so I 'll bolt you!
[*Dances round the room.*

Granny. Oh, mercy! murder! what is this I see?
Some frightful specter must the monster be!

Wolf. Do n't make a noise, for you 're a hopeless hobble in;
I 'm not a ghost, but soon shall be a gobble-in'!

[WOLF *flings himself on bed; shrieks and growls are heard. The dummy is removed without the audience being able to see it, as* WOLF *is in front of it.*

Wolf. [*Coming down*] Yahm! yahm! yahm! yahm! yahm!
I 've finished her ere she could angry be,
I did n't give her time to disagree with me.
Now for a night-gown [*takes one*] and a night-cap, [*takes one*] good! [*Puts them on.*
How do I look as Grandma Riding-hood?

[*Gets into bed, and covers himself up. A knock is heard at the door.*

Wolf. [*Imitating* GRANNY'S *voice*] Who 's there?

R. R. H. Your little grandchild, granny dear;
I have a cake and butter for you here.

Wolf. Pull at the bobbin, and the latch will rise.

[*Enter* R. R. H.

R. R. H. Good morning, granny! Here are the supplies. [*Sets down the basket.*

Wolf. Good morning, dear; come sit beside my bed. [R. R. H. *sits on the side of bed.*
I 'm very bad indeed, child, in my head.

R. R. H. Why granny, what big ears you 've got!

Wolf. My dear,
That is that granny may the better hear.

R. R. H. And, granny, what big eyes you 've got!

Wolf. Dear me!
That is that granny may the better see.

R. R. H. Then, granny, what big teeth you 've got! Oh, la!

Wolf. To eat you up with all the better. [*Springs out of bed and strikes an attitude*] Ha!

[R. R. H. *screams and runs away*, WOLF *pursues her round the table. Enter* JACK.

Jack. As I was passing by, I just dropt in.
[*To* WOLF] Shall I drop into you?

Wolf. Oh, pray begin!

Jack. You hideous brute, your wicked game I 'll stop. [*Hits* WOLF *with ax.*
How do you like that, monster?

Wolf. That 's first chop!

Jack. That is n't all—another chop to follow!
[*Strikes him again. They struggle.* WOLF *falls with a loud cry.*
Do n't hollo, sir!

Wolf. I must—I 'm beaten hollow;
You 've felled me to the earth.

Jack. Yes, I 'm the feller!
I 'll beat you black and blue.

Wolf. [*Aside*] Then I 'll turn yeller!
[*Goes into convulsions, shrieks, and feigns to be dead.* JACK *flings down ax, and embraces* R. R. H.

R. R. H. You 've saved my life, dear Jack! What can I do
To show my love and gratitude to you?

Jack. Sweetest Red Riding-hood, say you 'll be mine, [WOLF *creeps behind and secures ax.*
To jine our hands the parson I 'll enjine.

Wolf. [*Leaping up*] That en-gine won't assist you, tender pair;
If that 's your line, why I shall raise the fare.
[*Snatches up* R. R. H. *with one arm, brandishing ax.*

Jack. He 's got the ax—Oh, here 's a nice quandary!

R. R. H. You 'll raise the fare? [*Claps her hands.*
Then I will raise the Fairy!

[FAIRY *appears at the back. Enter the* MOTHER.

Mother. You wicked child, where have you been? Oho!
You 're listening to the shoot of that young beau!
But I forbid it, and I 'll have my way.

[FAIRY *comes forward.*

Fairy. Excuse me, but your orders I gainsay.

Mother. And who are you, ma'am, I should like to know?

Fairy. If you 'll be patient, time will quickly show.—
I come, Red Riding-hood, to give you aid;
But for a short space you must masquerade—
Partly as penance, part because it 's time
When little folks expect a pantomime.
[*To* JACK] With Jack, the wood-cutter, I will begin,
And change him into spangled Harlequin.
[*To* R. R. H.] While you, Red Riding-hood, awhile shall shine
As slippery, tripping, pretty Columbine.
[*To* MOTHER] I told you you would learn my business soon;

Now learn your own as silly Pantaloon.
[*To* WOLF] While you, with fit reward your deeds to crown,
I change to foolish, flapping, filching Clown!
[*Transformation; red fire, etc.*

Clown. Hullo! Here we are again!

COMIC BUSINESS.

SCENE:—*A street with shops. Enter* HARLEQUIN *and* COLUMBINE. *Dance and exit.*

Enter CLOWN, *who goes to Butcher's shop, followed by* PANTALOON, *and tries to steal a leg of mutton. Butcher sees him and hides, and then hits* CLOWN. CLOWN *turns round and knocks down* PANTALOON. PANTALOON *explains by signs that he did n't do it.* CLOWN *picks him up.* PANTALOON *engages Butcher in conversation, while* CLOWN *steals a round of beef, and tries to put it in his pocket; but it flies up and disappears at the touch of* HARLEQUIN'S *wand, who comes in at back.*

Clown. Hullo! There 's a rise in butcher's meat!

He then goes to Baker's shop, and steals a loaf, which disappears in the same way as the beef.

Clown. Oh, my! Bread 's a goin' up!

Servant-girl comes out of a house and begins to clean the steps. CLOWN *and* PANTALOON *both make love to her. She drives them off with her broom.* CLOWN *pushes* PANTALOON *backward into the pail. After helping him out, he takes the pail and washes his face in it, and then drinks the water. He then kisses Servant, who screams.*

Enter Policeman. CLOWN *makes signs that it was* PANTALOON. *While Policeman is taking* PANTALOON *in custody,* CLOWN *goes off and brings a red-hot poker. He walks on the other side of* PANTALOON, *and touches up Policeman with the hot end. Policeman shrieks and exit.* CLOWN *and* PANTALOON *run off in the opposite direction.*

Enter HARLEQUIN *and* COLUMBINE. *Dance.*

Enter CLOWN *and* PANTALOON *in pursuit trying to catch them.* COLUMBINE *dances off. They take* HARLEQUIN *by hands; they spin round, and then* HARLEQUIN *dodges under their arms and gets off, giving each a slap on the face.*

Enter a Peddler with a basket of fruit, a Fishmonger, and Baker with rolls. CLOWN *and* PANTALOON *trip them up; general row and pelting.*

Enter Policeman and drives them all off. CLOWN *hides in a shop, and comes out with some butter; licks it, and greases his hair with it.* PANTALOON *asks for a taste.* CLOWN *gets red-hot poker, and suddenly substituting it for the butter, burns* PANTALOON'S *tongue. While laughing at* PANTALOON, *he inadvertently takes hold of wrong end of poker and burns himself. Recommends* PANTALOON *to go to the Doctor. As soon as he has gone in,* CLOWN *makes a butter-slide on the steps, and knocks loudly at the door.* PANTALOON *and Doctor rush out, and both fall down. They threaten* CLOWN, *who jumps through Doctor's window. Doctor follows him, and* CLOWN *running out of the door, tumbles down on his own slide. Jumps up and hides. The Doctor comes out and rushes off in pursuit.* CLOWN *goes in and steals a lot of pill-boxes and bottles; he and* PANTALOON *sit down in front to share them. Enter* HARLEQUIN, *who comes behind and tickles* CLOWN, *who thinks it is* PANTALOON, *and knocks him over. They then sit down again to share plunder.*

Enter Doctor, who shakes his fist at them, and fetches in Policeman, who quietly sits down between them. As fast as CLOWN *has been giving* PANTALOON *his share in front, he has reached behind him and stolen it. As he is putting down something, he happens to look up and see Policeman. Terror; he slides away and bolts off the stage;* PANTALOON *follows, closely pursued by Policeman.*

Enter HARLEQUIN *and* COLUMBINE. *Dance.*

Stage gradually darkens; music ceases; they begin to grope about in the dark; CLOWN *steals* HARLEQUIN'S *bat, and he and* PANTALOON *take him prisoner.*

Scene changes to Transformation. FAIRY *discovered. Colored fires. The Characters form a group.*

Fairy. You 've had enough of frolic and of fun,
Your troubles end, the Pantomime is done.

[*To audience*] To you, kind friends, our grateful
thanks are due;
We 've done to please you all that we could do.
To pardon faults, we pray your condescension,
And ask your hands to mark our good intention.

COSTUMES.

JACK.—First dress: Coarse blouse, with belt; cap. Second dress: *Harlequin* outfit, consisting of ornamented tights, like those worn by circus actors.

THE WOLF.—First dress: Wolf mask; rough shawl or jacket; brown gloves. Second dress: As *Clown*, like the circus clown, with figured tights, and whitened face.

DAME MARGERY.—First dress: A flowered gown, tucked up all round, showing a quilted petticoat, or balmoral; cap with frill. Second dress: Tub-jacket of orange, made very full, with a prominent ruffle all round the waist; full breeches of same; red stockings; yellow shoes; long white beard and hair; red nose.

RED RIDING-HOOD.—First dress: Ordinary frock; scarlet hood. Second dress: White tarlatan, with spangles; red flowers in the hair.

THE FAIRY.—See description of Titania's dress on page 40.

THE OTHERS who appear in the Pantomime must, of course, dress in character.

REMARKS AND SUGGESTIONS.

This piece may be performed without the Comic Business, if desirable, but we would recommend the Pantomime to those who like broad fun. Nor is it difficult to get up. The scenery and properties for the drama proper are easily prepared. The transformation scene should represent a fairy grotto, and be made very gay and sparkling. The first dresses of the principal characters should be worn over the second, and so contrived that they may be undone and thrown off suddenly, with some assistance from the wings. The properties for the Comic Business must be made of muslin, stuffed and painted. It does not require much ingenuity to give them some resemblance in shape and color to pats of butter, fish, rounds of beef, and loaves. The loaf and round of beef, which go up, must be attached to a string, running through a ring somewhere at the top of the theater, and pulled by the prompter. The poker can either be painted red, or rubbed while warm with red sealing-wax. For the comic scene, a clothes horse or two will be found to make a good stable foundation for scenery. When covered with paper, and painted to represent shop-fronts, it can be stood in such a way as to allow the clown to jump through the window without tumbling down.

The part of granny is to be read by the prompter, who also aids in getting rid of the dummy. The butterfly, in Scene II., is affixed to a wire held at the wings.

Of course the clown's part should be assigned to a comic genius. Dame Margery is to be played by a boy.

LADY PENTWEAZEL AT THE ARTIST'S.

From Foote's Taste.

PERSONS REPRESENTED.

LADY PENTWEAZEL. MR. CARMINE. BOY.

SCENE:—CARMINE'S *Studio. An easel, with canvas; several portraits on the wall. Enter* CARMINE, *followed by* BOY.

Car. Lay these colors in the window, by the pallet. Any visitors, or messages?

Boy. A message from my Lady Pen—I can't remember her name, but 't is upon the slate.

Car. Let 's see,—[*Takes slate*] Oh! Lady Pentweazel, from Blow-bladder Street,—Admit her by all means! [*Exit* BOY] Lady Pentweazel! ha, ha! Now here 's a proof that avarice is not the only or last passion old age is subject to—this superannuated beldame gapes for flattery, like a nest of unfledged crows for food; and, like them, too, gulps down everything that 's offered her—no matter how coarse. Well, she shall be fed.. [*Enter* BOY.

Boy. Sir, my Lady Pen—

Car. Show her up stairs.

[*Enter* LADY PENTWEAZEL. *She glances at the pictures.*

Lady P. Fine pieces! very likely pieces! And, indeed, all alike. Hum! Lady Fussack—and, ha, ha, ha! Lady Glumstead, by all that 's ugly.—Pray now, Mr. Carmine, how do you contrive to overlook the ugliness, and yet preserve the likeness?

Car. The art, madam, may be conveyed in two words: where nature has been severe, we soften; where she has been kind, we aggravate.

Lady P. Very ingenus, and very kind, truly. Well, good sir, I bring you a subject that will demand the whole of the first part of your skill: and, if you are at leisure, you may begin directly.

Car. Your ladyship is here a little ungrateful to nature, and cruel to yourself; even Lady Pentweazel's enemies (if such there be) must allow that she is a fine woman.

Lady P. Oh, your servant, good sir! Why, I have had my day, Mr. Carmine; I have had my day.

Car. And have still, madam. The only difference I shall make between what you were and what you are, will be no more than what Rubens has distinguished between Mary de Medicis and a regent.

Lady P. Mr. Carmine, I vow you are a very judicious person; I was always said to be like that family. When my piece was first done, the limner did me after Venus de Medicis, which, I suppose, might be one of Mary's sisters: but things must change; to be sitting for my picture at this time of day—ha, ha, ha! But my daughter Sukey, you must know, is just married to Mr. Deputy Dripping, of Candlewick-ward, and would not be said nay; so it is not so much for the beauty, as the similitude.—Ha, ha, ha!

Car. True, madam: ha, ha, ha! But if I hit the likeness, I must preserve the beauty. Will your ladyship be seated? [*She sits.*

Lady P. I have heard, good sir, that every body has a more betterer and more worser side of the face than the other—now which will you choose?

Car. The right side, madam,—the left—now, if you please, the full.—Your ladyship's countenance is so exactly proportioned that I must have it all, no feature can be spared.

Lady P. When you come to the eyes, Mr. Carmine, let me know, that I may call up a look.

Car. Mighty well, madam! your face a little nearer to the left, nearer me—your head more up—shoulders back—and chest forward.

Lady P. Bless me, Mr. Carmine, do n't mind my shape this bout; for I am only in jumps. Shall I send for my tabbies?

Car. No, madam, we'll supply that for the present.—Your ladyship was just now mentioning a daughter.—Is she—your face a little more toward me—Is she the sole inheritor of her mother's beauty? Or, have you—

Lady P. That? ha, ha, ha! Why, that is my youngest of all, except Caleb.

Car. Now, madam, I am come to the eyes—Oh, that look—that—that I must despair of imitating.

Lady P. Oh, oh, good sir! Have you found out that? Why, all my family, by the mother's side, were famous for their eyes: I have a great aunt among the beauties of Windsor: She has a sister at Hampton-court, a perdigious fine woman—she had but one eye, indeed, but that was a piercer; that one eye got her three husbands—we were called the gimlet-eyed family. Oh, Mr. Carmine; you need not mind these heats in my face; they always discharge themselves about Christmas—my true carnation is not seen in my countenance. That 's carnation! Here 's your flesh and blood.

[*Showing her arm.*

Car. Delicate, indeed! finely turned, and of a charming color!

Lady P. And yet it has been employed enough to spoil the best hand and arm in the world—even before marriage never idle; none of your galloping, gossiping, Ranelagh romps, like the forward minxes of the present age. I was always employed, either in painting your lamskips, playing upon the harpsicols, making paste, or something or other.—All our family had a geno: and then I sung! Every body said I had a monstrous fine voice for music.

Car. That may be discerned by your ladyship's tones in conversation.

Lady P. Tones! you are right, Mr. Carmine; that was Mr. Purcell's word. Miss Polly Grisken, says he (my maiden name), you have tones.

Car. Inimitable ones.

Lady P. But, Mr. Carmine, you limners are all ingenus men—you sing?

Car. A ballad, or so, madam; music is a sister art; and it would be a little unnatural not to cultivate an acquaintance there.

Lady P. Why, truly, we ought not to be ashamed of our relations, unless they are poor;—and then, you know,— [*Enter* BOY.

Boy. Alderman Pentweazel and Mr. Puff.

Lady P. Oh, he was to call upon me; we go to the auction. Good day.

[*Exit, followed by* CARMINE, *bowing with mock respect.*

COSTUMES.

CARMINE.—Ordinary modern suit.

LADY PENTWEAZEL.—Gaudy outfit, overloaded with inappropriate ornaments; curls; gold watch; fan; etc.

SUGGESTION.

Lady Pentweazel should be painted and "made up" so as to appear as course, florid, and ugly as possible. Her attitudes and gestures should be awkward and affected; her voice harsh and disagreeable. The part may be taken, with amusing effect, by a gentleman dressed in female costume.

THE DISCOMFITED RIVALS.

From Wycherly's Plain Dealer.

PERSONS REPRESENTED.

LORD PLAUSIBLE, *a noble coxcomb.* NOVEL, *his rival in love.*
BOY.

SCENE:—*A Drawing-room. Enter* R. LORD PLAUSIBLE *and* BOY.

L. Plaus. (C.) Little gentleman, your most obedient, faithful, humble servant: where, I beseech you, where is that divine person, your noble lady?

Boy. (R. C.) Gone out, my lord; but commanded me to give you this letter.

[*Gives him a letter. Enter* NOVEL.

L. Plaus. [*Aside*] Which he must not observe.

[*Puts it up.*

Novel. Hey, boy, where is thy lady?

Boy. Gone out, sir; but I must beg a word with you. [*Gives him a letter, and exit* R.

Novel. For me? So! [*Puts up the letter*] Servant, servant, my lord; you see the lady knew of your coming, for she is gone out.

L. Plaus. Sir, I humbly beseech you not to censure the lady's good breeding: she has reason to use more liberty with me than with any other man.

Novel. How, viscount, how?

L. Plaus. Nay, I humbly beseech you, be not in choler; where there is most love there may be most freedom.

Novel. Nay, then, 't is time to come to an explanation with you, and to tell you, you must think no more of this lady's love.

L. Plaus. Why, under correction, dear sir?

Novel. There are reasons, reasons, viscount.

L. Plaus. What, I beseech you, noble sir.

Novel. Pr'ythee, pr'ythee, be not impertinent, my lord; some of you lords are such conceited, well-assured, impertinent rogues—

L. Plaus. And you noble wits are so full of shamming and drolling, one knows not when to have you seriously.

Novel. Pr'ythee, my lord, be not an ass: dost thou think to get this lady from me? I have had such good encouragements—

L. Plaus. I have not been thought unworthy of them.

Novel. What, not like mine! Come to an explanation, as I said.

L. Plaus. Why, seriously, then, she has told me viscountess sounded prettily.

Novel. And me, that Novel was a name she would sooner change her's for, than for any title in England.

L. Plaus. She has commended the softness and respectfulness of my behavior.

Novel. She has praised the briskness of my raillery, of all things, man.

L. Plaus. The sleepiness of my eyes she commended.

Novel. Sleepiness! dullness, dullness! But the fierceness of mine she adored.

L. Plaus. The brightness of my hair she liked.

Novel. The brightness! no, the greasiness, I warrant; but the blackness and the luster of mine she admires.

L. Plaus. The gentleness of my smile.

Novel. The subtlety of my leer.

L. Plaus. The clearness of my complexion.

Novel. The redness of my lips.

L. Plaus. Well, sir, to put you out of all doubt, she has received some jewels from me of value.

Novel. And presents from me.

L. Plaus. Nay, then, sir, with your favor, and to make an end of all your hopes, look you here, sir,—she has writ to me.

Novel. How! How! well, well, and so she has to me; look you there. [*Exchange letters.*

L. Plaus. What's here?

Novel. How's this? [*Reads out.*

"My Dear Lord:

"*You'll excuse me for breaking my word with you, since 't was to oblige, not to offend you; for I am only gone abroad but to disappoint Novel, and meet you in the drawing-room; where I expect you with as much impatience as when I used to suffer Novel's visits, the most impertinent fop that ever affected the name of a wit, therefore not capable, I hope, to give you jealousy; for, for your sake alone, you saw I renounced an old lover, and will do all the world. Burn the letter, but lay up the kindness of it in your heart, with your*

"OLIVIA."

Very fine! but pray, let 's see mine.

L. Plaus. I understand it not. But sure, she can not think so of me.

[*Reads the other letter aloud, and hands it to* NOVEL.

Novel. Humph! hah!—"*Meet—for your sake*"—umph—"*quitted an old lover—world—burn—in your heart, with your* OLIVIA."

Just the same, the names only altered.

L. Plaus. Surely there must be some mistake; or somebody has abused her and us.

Novel. Yes, you are abused, no doubt of it, my lord, but I'll to Whitehall and see.

L. Plaus. And I, when I shall find you are abused.

Novel. Where, if it be so, for our comfort, we can not fail of meeting with fellow-sufferers enough; for, as Freeman said of another, she stands in the drawing-room, like a glass, ready for all comers to set their gallantry by her: and, like the glass, too, lets no man go from her unsatisfied with himself.

[*Exeunt*, R.

COSTUMES.

LORD PLAUSIBLE.—Doublet of silk or velvet, with large loose sleeves slashed up the front, the collar covered with lace; short cloak on one shoulder; long breeches, fringed or pointed; wide boots, ruffled at top with lace or lawn; broad-brimmed felt hat, with rich band, and plume of feathers; Spanish rapier hung from showy sword-belt, worn sash-wise over right shoulder; curls and powdered wig, peaked beard, small up-turned mustaches.

NOVEL.—In the same fashion as the above, but differing enough to afford a pleasant contrast.

SUGGESTIONS.

The manner of Lord Plausible should be very ceremonious; his speech drawling and affected. Novel must appear pert, dashing, and vivacious. In the contrast of the two characters lies much of the interest of the dialogue and action.

THE MOCK DOCTOR.

Translated from the French by Fielding.

PERSONS REPRESENTED.

SIR JASPER.	GREGORY.	CHARLOTTE.
JAMES.	LEANDER.	MAID.

SCENE:—SIR JASPER'S *house.* *Enter* SIR JASPER *and* JAMES.

Sir Jasper. Where is he? Where is he?

James. Only recruiting himself after his long journey. You need not be impatient, sir; for were my young lady dead, he'd bring her to life again.

He makes no more of bringing a patient to life, than other physicians do of killing him.

Sir Jasper. 'T is strange so great a man should have those odd humors you mentioned.

James. 'T is but a good blow or two, and he comes immediately to himself.—Here he is. [*Enter* GREGORY] Sir, this is the doctor.

Sir Jasper. Dear sir, you 're the welcomest man in the world.

Gre. Hippocrates says we should both be covered.

Sir Jasper. Ha! does Hippocrates say so? In what chapter, pray.

Gre. In his chapter of hats.

Sir Jasper. Since Hippocrates says so, I shall obey him.

Gre. Doctor, after having exceedingly traveled in the highway of letters—

Sir Jasper. Doctor! Pray, whom do you speak to?

Gre. To you, doctor.

Sir Jasper. Ha, ha, ha! I am a knight, thank the king's grace for it; but no doctor.

Gre. What, you 're no doctor?

Sir Jasper. No, upon my word!

Gre. You 're no doctor?

Sir Jasper. Doctor! No.

Gre. There—'t is done. [*Beats him.*

Sir Jasper. Done, in the name of wonder! What 's done?

Gre. Why, now you are made a doctor of physic—I am sure 't is all the degree I ever took.

Sir Jasper. What idiot of a fellow have you brought here?

James. I told you, sir, the doctor had strange whims with him.

Sir Jasper. Whims, quotha! Egad, I shall bind his physicianship over to his good behavior, if he has any more of these whims.

Gre. Sir, I ask pardon for the liberty I have taken.

Sir Jasper. Oh! 't is very well, 't is very well for once.

Gre. I am sorry for those blows—

Sir Jasper. Nothing at all, nothing at all, sir.

Gre. Which I was obliged to have the honor of laying on so thick upon you.

Sir Jasper. Let 's talk no more of them, sir.—My daughter, doctor, is fallen into a very strange distemper.

Gre. Sir, I am overjoyed to hear it; and I wish, with all my heart, you and your whole family had the same occasion for me as your daughter, to show the great desire I have to serve you.

Sir Jasper. Sir, I am obliged to you.

Gre. I assure you, sir, I speak from the very bottom of my soul.

Sir Jasper. I do believe you, sir, from the very bottom of mine.

Gre. What is your daughter's name?

Sir Jasper. My daughter's name is Charlotte.

Gre. Are you sure she was christened Charlotte?

Sir Jasper. No, sir; she was christened Charlotta.

Gre. Hum! I had rather she should have been Charlotte. Charlotte is a very good name for a patient; and, let me tell you, the name is often of as much service to a patient as the physician is.

Sir Jasper. Sir, my daughter is here.

[*Enter* CHARLOTTE *and* MAID.

Gre. Is that my patient? Upon my word she carries no distemper in her countenance.

Sir Jasper. You make her smile, doctor.

Gre. So much the better; 't is a very good sign when we can bring a patient to smile; it is a sign that the distemper begins to clarify, as we say.—Well, child, what 's the matter with you? What 's your distemper?

Char. Han, hi, hon, han.

Gre. What do you say?

Char. Han, hi, hon, han.

Gre. What, what, what?—

Char. Han, hi, hon—

Gre. Han! hon! honin! ha? I do n't understand a word she says. Han! hi! hon! What sort of a language is this!

Sir Jasper. Why, that 's her distemper, sir. She 's become dumb, and no one can assign the cause—and this distemper, sir, has kept back her marriage.

Gre. Kept back her marriage! Why so?

Sir Jasper. Because her lover refuses to have her till she 's cured.

Gre. Oh, lud! Was ever such a fool, that would not have his wife dumb?—Would to Heaven my wife was dumb, I 'd be far from desiring to cure her!—Does this distemper, this han, hi, hon, oppress her very much?

Sir Jasper. Yes, sir.

Gre. All the better. Has she any great pain?

Sir Jasper. Very great.

Gre. That 's just as I would have it. Give me your hand, child. Hum—ha—a very dumb pulse indeed.

Sir Jasper. You have guessed her distemper.

Gre. Ay, sir, we great physicians know a distemper immediately: I know some of the college would call this the boree, or the coupee, or the sinkee, or twenty other distempers; but I give you my word, sir, your daughter is nothing more than dumb.—So I 'd have you be very easy, for there is nothing else the matter with her.—If she were not dumb, she would be as well as I am.

Sir Jasper. But I should be glad to know, doctor, from whence her dumbness proceeds?

Gre. Nothing so easily accounted for.—Her dumbness proceeds from her having lost her speech.

Sir Jasper. But whence, if you please, proceeds her having lost her speech?

Gre. All the best authors will tell you it is the impediment of the action of the tongue.

Sir Jasper. But if you please, dear sir, your sentiments upon that impediment?

Gre. Aristotle has, upon that subject, said very fine things; very fine things.

Sir Jasper. I believe it, doctor.

Gre. Ah! he was a great man; he was indeed a very great man—a man, who, upon that subject, was a man that—But, to return to our reasoning; I hold that this impediment of the action of the tongue is caused by certain humors, which our great physicians call—Humors—Humors—Ah! you understand Latin?

Sir Jasper. Not in the least.

Gre. What! not understand Latin?

Sir Jasper. No, indeed, doctor.

Gre. Cubricius arci thurum cathalimus, singularitur nom. Hæc musa: hic, hæc, hoc, genitivo hujus, hunc, hanc, musæ. Bonus, bona, bonum. Estne oratio Latinus? Etiam. Quia substantivo et adjectivum concordat in generi numerum et casus, sic dicunt, aiunt, prædicant, claimitant, et similibus.

Sir Jasper. Ah! why did I neglect my studies?

James. What a prodigious man is this!

Gre. Besides, sir, certain spirits passing from the left side, which is the seat of the liver, to the right, which is the seat of the heart, we find the lungs, which we call in Latin *whiskerus*, having communication with the brain, which we name in Greek *jacbootos*, by means of a hollow vein, which we call in Hebrew *periwiggus*, meet in the road with said spirits, which fill the ventricles of the omotaplasmus; and because the said humors have—you comprehend me well, sir? and because the said humors have a certain malignity—listen seriously, I beg you.

Sir Jasper. I do.

Gre. Have a certain malignity that is caused—be attentive, if you please.

Sir Jasper. I am.

Gre. That is caused, I say, by the acrimony of the humors engendered in the concavity of the diaphragm; thence it arrives, that these vapors, *Propria quæ maribus tribuuntur mascula, dicas, ut sunt divorum, Mars, Bacchus, Appollo, virorum.* This, sir, is the cause of your daughter's being dumb.

James. Oh, that I had his tongue!

Sir Jasper. It is impossible to reason better, no doubt. But, dear sir, there is one thing—I always thought, till now, that the heart was on the left side, and the liver on the right.

Gre. Ay, sir, so they were formerly; but we have changed all that. The college at present, sir, proceeds on an entire new method.

Sir Jasper. I ask your pardon, sir.

Gre. Oh, sir! there's no harm—you're not obliged to know as much as we do.

Sir Jasper. Very true; but, doctor, what would you have done with my daughter?

Gre. What would I have done with her? Why, my advice is, that you immediately put her into a bed warmed with a brass warming-pan: cause her to drink one quart of spring water, mixed with one pint of brandy, six Seville oranges, and three ounces of the best double refined sugar.

Sir Jasper. Why, this is punch, doctor?

Gre. Punch, sir! ay, sir; and what 's better than punch to make people talk? Never tell me of your julaps, your gruels, your—your—your—this, and that, and 'tother, which are only arts to keep a patient in hand a long time—I love to do a business all at once.

Sir Jasper. Doctor, I ask pardon; you shall be obeyed. [*Gives money.*

Gre. I 'll return in the evening, and see what effect it has on her. But hold; there 's another young lady here that I must apply some little remedy to.

Maid. Who, me? I was never better in my life, thank you, sir.

Gre. So much the worse, madam; so much the worse. 'T is very dangerous to be very well; for when one is very well, one has nothing else to do but to take physic and bleed away.

Sir Jasper. Oh, strange! What, bleed when one has no distemper?

Gre. It may be strange, perhaps, but it is very wholesome. Besides, madam, it is not your case at present to be very well: at least you can not possibly be well above three days longer; and it is always best to cure a distemper before you have it—or, as we say in Greek, *distemprum bestum est curare ante habestum.* What I shall prescribe you at present is to take every six hours one of these bolusses.

Maid. Ha, ha, ha! Why, doctor, these look exactly like lumps of loaf-sugar.

Gre. Take one of these bolusses, I say, every six hours, washing it down with six spoonfuls of the best Holland's Geneva.

Sir Jasper. Sure you are in jest, doctor; this girl does not show any symptoms of a distemper.

Gre. Sir Jasper, let me tell you, it were not amiss if you yourself took a little lenitive physic; I shall prepare something for you.

Sir Jasper. Ha, ha, ha! No! no, doctor! I have escaped both doctors and distempers hitherto, and I am resolved the distemper shall pay me the first visit.

Gre. Say you so, sir? Why, then, if I can get no more patients here, I must even seek them elsewhere; and so humbly beggo to domine domitii, remain groundi foras. 'But, by your leave, before I 'go, I would communicate a word in private to my 'amiable patient.'

Sir Jasper. 'Certainly. [*Aside*] This is a phys- 'ician of vast capacity, but of exceeding odd humors.'

[*Exit* SIR JASPER *and* MAID.

Gre. [*Producing a letter*] 'And now, my dear, 'here is a prescription that I think will be to your 'liking. To-morrow I will bring Leander himself, 'disguised as an apothecary. While I then engage

'Sir Jasper in conversation Leander may run away 'with you, and thus Dapper will be cheated.'

Char. 'Oh, you dear old, cunning, rogue.'

Gre. 'Hush! You can't speak until to-morrow. 'Until then, only hi—ho, hon.—Adieu.' [*Exit.*

Char. 'Oh, dear, what a torment it is to a woman 'to be obliged to hold her tongue.' [*Exit.*

SCENE II:—*The same. Enter* SIR JASPER, CHARLOTTE *and* MAID.

Sir Jasper. Has she made no attempt to speak yet?

Maid. Not in the least, sir; so far from it, that, as she used to make a sort of a noise before, she is now quite silent.

Sir Jasper. [*Looking on his watch*] 'T is almost the time the doctor promised to return.—Oh, he is here! Doctor, your servant.

[*Enter* GREGORY *and* LEANDER.

Gre. Well, sir, how does my patient?

Sir Jasper. Rather worse, sir, since your prescription.

Gre. So much the better; 't is a sign that it operates.

Sir Jasper. Who is that gentleman, pray, with you?

Gre. An apothecary, sir.—Mr. Apothecary, I desire you would immediately apply that song I prescribed.

Sir Jasper. A song, doctor! Prescribe a song?

Gre. Prescribe a song, sir! Yes, sir; prescribe a song, sir. Is there any thing so strange in that? Did you never hear of pills to purge melancholy? If you understand these things better than I, why did you send for me? Sure, sir, this song would make a stone speak. But, if you please, sir, you and I will confer at some distance during the application; for this song will do you as much harm as it will do your daughter good. Be sure, Mr. Apothecary, to pour it down her ears very closely.

Leander. *Thus, lovely patient, Charlotte sees*
Her dying patient kneel;
Soon cured will be your feigned disease;
But what physician e'er can ease
The torments which I feel?
Think, charming nymph, while I complain;
Ah, think what I endure!
All other remedies are vain;
The lovely cause of all my pain
Can only cause my cure.

Gre. [*To* SIR JASPER] It is, sir, a great and subtle question among the doctors, whether women are more easy to be cured than men? I beg you would attend to this, sir, if you please—Some say, No; others say, Yes; and, for my part, I say both Yes and No; forasmuch as the incongruity of the opaque humors that meet in the natural tempers of women, are the cause that the brutal part will always prevail over the sensible.—One sees that the inequality of their opinions depends upon the black movement of the circle of the moon; and as the sun, that darts his rays upon the concavity of the earth—

Char. No, I am not at all capable of changing my opinion.

Sir Jasper. My daughter speaks! my daughter speaks! Oh, the great power of physic! oh, the admirable physician! How can I reward thee for such a service?

Gre. This distemper has given me a most insufferable deal of trouble.

[*Traversing the stage in a great heat, the apothecary following.*

Char. Yes, sir, I have recovered my speech; but I have recovered it to tell you that I never will have any husband but Leander.

[*Speaks with great eagerness, and drives* SIR JASPER *round the stage.*

Sir Jasper. But—

Char. Nothing is capable to shake the resolution I have taken.

Sir Jasper. What!

Char. Your rhetoric is in vain; all your discourses signify nothing.

Sir Jasper. I—

Char. I am determined; and all the fathers in the world shall never oblige me to marry contrary to my inclinations.

Sir Jasper. I have—

Char. I will never submit to this tyranny; and if I must not have the man I like, I 'll die a maid.

Sir Jasper. You shall have Mr. Dapper—

Char. No,—not in any manner—not in the least; not at all! You throw away your breath; you lose your time: you may confine me, beat me, bruise me, destroy me, kill me; do what you will, use me as you will; but I never will consent; nor all your threats, nor all your blows, nor all your ill-usage, never shall force me to consent. So far from giving him my heart, I never will give him my hand: for he is my aversion; I hate the very sight of him; I had rather see a snake. I had rather touch a toad! You may make me miserable another way; but with him you sha'n't, that I 'm resolved!

Gre. There, sir, there! I think we have brought her tongue to a pretty tolerable consistency.

Sir Jasper. Consistency, quotha! why, there 's no stopping her tongue.—Dear doctor, I desire you would make her dumb again.

Gre. That 's impossible, sir. All that I can do to serve you is, I can make you deaf, if you please.

Sir Jasper. And do you think—

Char. All your reasoning shall never conquer my resolution.

Sir Jasper. You shall marry Mr. Dapper this evening.

Char. I 'll be buried first.

Gre. Stay, sir, stay! Let me regulate this affair;

it is a distemper that possesses her, and I know what remedy to apply to it.

Sir Jasper. Is it possible, sir, that you can cure the distemper of the mind?

Gre. Sir, I can cure anything. Hark ye, Mr. Apothecary! you see that the love she has for Leander is entirely contrary to the will of her father, and that there is no time to lose, and that an immediate remedy is necessary. For my part, I know of but one, which is a dose of purgative running away, mixed with two drams of pills matrimoniac; perhaps she will make some difficulty to take them; but as you are an able apothecary, I shall trust to you for the success. Go, make her walk in the garden; be sure lose no time; to the remedy quick; to the remedy specific!

[*Exeunt* LEANDER *and* CHARLOTTE.

Sir Jasper. What drugs, sir, were those I heard you mention, for I do n't remember I ever heard them spoke of before?

Gre. They are some, sir, lately discovered by the Royal Society.

Sir Jasper. Did you ever hear anything equal to her insolence?

Gre. Daughters are indeed sometimes a little too headstrong.

Sir Jasper. You can not imagine, sir, how foolishly fond she is of that Leander.

Gre. The heat of blood, sir, causes that in young minds.

Sir Jasper. For my part, from the moment I discovered the violence of her passion, I have always kept her locked up.

Gre. You have done very wisely.

Sir Jasper. And I have prevented them from having the least communication together; for who knows what might have been the consequence? Who knows but she might have taken it into her head to have run away with him.

Gre. Very true.

Sir Jasper. Ay, sir, let me alone for governing girls; I think I have some reason to be vain on that head; I think I have shown the world that I understand a little of women—I think, I have; and, let me tell you, sir, there is not a little art required. If this girl had had some fathers, they had not kept her out of the hands of so vigilant a lover as I have done.

Gre. No, certainly not. [*Enter* JAMES.

James. Oh, sir, undone, undone! your daughter is run away with her lover Leander, who was here disguised like an apothecary—and this is the rogue of a physician who has contrived all the affair.

Sir Jasper. How! am I abused in this manner? Here! who is there? Bid my clerk bring pen, ink, and paper; I 'll send this fellow to jail immediately.

James. Indeed, my good doctor, you stand a very fair chance to be hanged for stealing an heiress.

Gre. Yes, indeed, I believe I shall take my degree now. [*Enter* LEANDER *and* CHARLOTTE.

Leander. Behold, sir, that Leander, whom you had forbid your house, restores your daughter to your power, even when he had her in his. I will receive her, sir, only at your hands.—I have received letters, by which I have learned of the death of an uncle, whose estate far exceeds that of your intended son-in-law.

Sir Jasper. Sir, your virtue is beyond all estates; and I give you my daughter with all the pleasure in the world.

Leander. Now my fortune makes me happy indeed, my dearest Charlotte! and, doctor, I'll make thy fortune, too.

Gre. If you would be so kind as to make me a physician in earnest, I should desire no other fortune.

Leander. Faith, doctor, I wish I could do that in return for your having made me an apothecary; but I'll do as well for thee, I'll warrant.

Sir Jasper. May I beg to know whether you are a physician or not?

Gre. I think, sir, after the miraculous cure you have seen me perform, you have no reason to ask whether I am a physician or not.

SONG.

When tender young virgins look pale and complain,
You may send for a dozen great doctors in vain;
All give their opinion, and pocket their fees;

Each writes her a cure, though all miss her disease;
Powders, drops,
Julaps, slops,
A cargo of poison from physical shops.

Though they physic to death the unhappy poor maid,
What's that to the doctor—since he must be paid?
Would you know how you may manage her right?
Our doctor has brought you a nostrum to-night,
Can never vary
Nor miscarry,
If the lover be but the apothecary.

SENTIMENTALITY.

From Steele's Tender Husband.

PERSONS REPRESENTED.

AUNT TIPKIN. MISS BRIDGET.

SCENE:—*A Sitting-room. Enter* AUNT *and* NIECE.

Niece. Was it not my gallant that whistled so charmingly in the parlor before he went out this morning? He 's a most accomplished cavalier.

Aunt. Come, niece, come—You do n't do well to make sport with your relations, especially with a young gentleman that has so much kindness for you.

Niece. Kindness for me! What a phrase is there to express the darts and flames, the sighs and languishings of an expecting lover!

Aunt. Pray, niece, forbear this idle trash, and talk like other people. Your cousin Humphrey will be true and hearty in what he says, and that 's a great deal better than the talk and compliment of romances.

Niece. Good madam, do n't wound my ears with such expressions. Do you think I can ever love a man that 's true and hearty? What a peasant-like amour do these coarse words import! True and hearty! Pray, aunt, endeavor a little at the embellishment of your style.

Aunt. Alack-a-day, cousin Biddy, these idle romances have quite turned your head.

Niece. How often must I desire you, madam, to lay aside that familiar name, cousin Biddy? I never hear it without blushing.—Did you ever meet with a heroine, in those idle romances as you call 'em, that was termed Biddy?

Aunt. Ah! cousin, cousin,—these are mere vapors indeed—Nothing but vapors—

Niece. No, the heroine has always something soft and engaging in her name—something that gives us a notion of the sweetness of her beauty and behavior. A name that glides through half a dozen tender syllables, as Elismunda, Clidamira, Deidamia; that runs upon vowels off the tongue, not hissing through one's teeth, or breaking them with consonants.—'T is strange rudeness, those familiar names they give us, when there is Aurelia, Saccharissa, Gloriana, for people of condition; and Celia, Chloris, Corinna, Mopsa, for their maids and those of lower rank.

Aunt. Look ye, Biddy, this is not to be supported—I know not where you learned this nicety; but I can tell you, forsooth, as much as you despise it, your mother was a Bridget afore you, and an excellent housewife.

Niece. Good madam, do n't upbraid me with my mother Bridget, and an excellent housewife.

Aunt. Yes, I say, she was, and spent her time in

better learning than ever you did—not in reading of fights and battles of dwarfs and giants; but in writing out receipts for broths, possets, caudles, and surfeit-waters, as became a good country gentlewoman.

Niece. My mother, and a Bridget!

Aunt. Yes, niece, I say again, your mother, my sister, was a Bridget! the daughter of her mother Margery, of her mother Cicely, of her mother Alice.

Niece. Have you no mercy? Oh, the barbarous genealogy!

Aunt. Of her mother Winifred, of her mother Joan.

Niece. Since you will run on, then I must needs tell you I am not satisfied in the point of my nativity. Many an infant has been placed in a cottage with obscure parents, till by chance some ancient servant of the family has known it by its marks.

Aunt. Ay, you had best be searched.—That 's like your calling the winds the fanning gales, before I do n't know how much company; and the tree that was blown by it, had, forsooth, a spirit imprisoned in the trunk of it.

Niece. Ignorance!

Aunt. Then a cloud this morning had a flying dragon in it.

Niece. What eyes had you that you could see nothing? For my part, I look upon it to be a prodigy, and expect something extraordinary will happen to me before night.—But you have a gross relish of things. What noble descriptions in romances had been lost, if the writers had been persons of your taste!

Aunt. I wish the authors had been hanged, and their books burnt, before you had seen 'em.

Niece. Simplicity!

Aunt. A parcel of improbable lies.

Niece. Indeed, madam, your raillery is coarse.

Aunt. Fit only to corrupt young girls, and fill their heads with a thousand foolish dreams of I do n't know what.

Niece. Nay, now, madam, you grow extravagant.

Aunt. What I say is, not to vex, but advise you for your good.

Niece. What, to burn Philocles, Artaxerxes, Oroondates, and the rest of the heroic lovers, and take my country booby, cousin Humphrey for a husband!

Aunt. Oh, dear, oh, dear, Biddy! Pray, good dear, learn to speak and act like the rest of the world: come, come, you shall marry your cousin, and live comfortably.

Niece. Live comfortably! What kind of life is that? A great heiress live comfortably! Pray, aunt, learn to raise your ideas.—What is, I wonder, to live comfortably?

Aunt. To live comfortably, is to live with prudence and frugality, as we do in Lombard street.

Niece. As we do.—That 's a fine life indeed, with one servant of each sex.—Let 's see how many things our coachman is good for.—He rubs down his horses, lays the cloth, whets the knives, and sometimes makes beds.

Aunt. A good servant should turn his hand to everything in a family.

Niece. Nay, there 's not a creature in our family that has not two or three different duties, as John is butler, footman, and coachman, so Mary is cook, laundress, and chambermaid.

Aunt. Well, and do you laugh at that?

Niece. No—not I—nor at the coach horses, though one has an easy trot for my uncle's riding, and t 'other an easy pace for your side-saddle.

Aunt. And so you sneer at the good management of your relations, do you?

Niece. No, I 'm well satisfied that all the house are creatures of business; but, indeed, I was in hopes that my poor lap-dog might have lived with me without an employment; but my uncle threatens every day to make him a turnspit, that he, too, in his sphere, may help us to live comfortably.

[*Crossing over.*

Aunt. Hark ye, cousin Biddy.

Niece. I vow I 'm out of countenance when our butler, with his careful face, drives us all stowed in a chariot, drawn by one horse ambling, and t 'other trotting with his provisions behind for the family, from Saturday night till Monday morning, bound for Hackney.—Then we make a comfortable figure indeed.

Aunt. So we do, and so will you always, if you marry your cousin Humphrey.

Niece. Name not the creature.

Aunt. Creature! What, your own cousin a creature!

Niece. Oh, let 's be going. I see yonder another creature that does my uncle's law business, and has, I believe, made ready the deeds, those barbarous deeds.

Aunt. What! Mr. Pounce, a creature, too! Nay, you 'll learn more wit from him in an hour, than in a thousand of your foolish books in a year.

[*Exeunt.*

THE FOREST EXILES.

From Shakespeare's As You Like It.

PERSONS REPRESENTED.

DUKE, *living in exile.*
AMIENS, } *Lords attending the Duke.*
JAQUES, }
ORLANDO, *lost in the forest.*
ADAM, *servant to Orlando.*
LORDS.

Prologue.

Notwithstanding its want of plot and action, Shakespeare's *As You Like It* is one of the most charming plays ever written. It is the very essence of romantic poetry. We have selected for your entertainment, some of the most pleasing passages of the Second Act, in which the banished duke and his friends in exile are represented losing "the creeping hours of time" in the Forest of Arden. "Nothing sweeter," says Taine, "than this mixture of tender compassion, dreamy philosophy, delicate sadness, poetical complaints, and rustic songs." The interest of our play depends almost entirely upon the wit and beauty of the speeches, not upon stage effects or startling declamation. Particular attention is called to the character of the melancholy

Jaques, his description of the "fool i' th' forest," and of the "seven ages" of man. These two noted speeches, and that descriptive of the wounded deer, are the principal gems in this cluster of poetic jewels.

SCENE I:—*The Forest of Arden. Enter* DUKE, AMIENS, *and two or three* LORDS, *in the dress of Foresters*, L.

Duke. (C.) Now, my co-mates, and brothers in exile,
Hath not old custom made this life more sweet
Than that of painted pomp? Are not these woods
More free from peril than the envious Court?
Here feel we but the penalty of Adam—
The seasons' difference; as, the icy fang
And churlish chiding of the winter's wind,
Which, when it bites and blows upon my body,
Even till I shrink with cold, I smile and say,
This is no flattery,—these are counsellors
That feelingly persuade me what I am.
Sweet are the uses of adversity,
Which, like the toad, ugly and venomous,
Wears yet a precious jewel in his head;
And this our life, exempt from public haunt,
Finds tongues in trees, books in the running brooks,
Sermons in stones, and good in every thing:
I would not change it.

Amiens. (R.) Happy is your Grace
That can translate the stubbornness of fortune
Into so quiet, and so sweet a style.

Duke. Come, shall we go and kill us venison?
And yet it irks me, the poor dappled fools,—
Being native burghers of this desert city,—
Should, in their own confines, with forked heads,
Have their round haunches gored.

1*st Lord.* (L.) Indeed, my lord,
The melancholy Jaques grieves at that;
And, in that kind, swears you do more usurp
Than doth your brother that hath banished you.
To-day, my Lord of Amiens and myself
Did steal behind him as he lay along
Under an oak, whose antique root peeps out
Upon the brook that brawls along this wood:
To the which place a poor sequestered stag,
That from the hunter's aim had ta'en a hurt,
Did come to languish; and, indeed, my lord,
The wretched animal heaved forth such groans
That their discharge did stretch his leathern coat
Almost to bursting; and the big round tears
Coursed one another down his innocent nose
In piteous chase: and thus the hairy fool,
Much marked of the melancholy Jaques,
Stood on the extremest verge of the swift brook,
Augmenting it with tears.

Duke. But what said Jaques?—
Did he not moralize this spectacle?

1*st Lord.* O yes, into a thousand similes.

First, for his weeping into th' needless stream;
"Poor deer," quoth he, "thou mak'st a testament
As worldlings do, giving thy sum of more
To that which had too much." Then, being there
alone,
Left and abandoned of his velvet friends;
"'T is right," quoth he; "thus misery doth part
The flux of company." Anon, a careless herd,
Full of the pasture, jumps along by him,
And never stays to greet him. "Ay," quoth Jaques,
"Sweep on, you fat and greasy citizens;
'T is just the fashion: wherefore do you look
Upon that poor and broken bankrupt there?"
Thus most invectively he pierceth through
The body of the country, city, court,
Yea, and of this our life: swearing that we
Are mere usurpers, tyrants, and what 's worse,
To fright the animals, and to kill them up
In their assigned and native dwelling-place.

Duke. And did you leave him in this contemplation?

2*d Lord.* We did, my lord, weeping and commenting
Upon the sobbing deer.

Duke. Show me the place;
I love to cope him in these sullen fits,
For then he 's full of matter.

1*st Lord.* I 'll bring you to him straight.

[*Exeunt*, L.

SCENE II:—*Another part of the Forest.* *Enter* ORLANDO *and* ADAM, L.

Adam. (L.) Dear master, I can go no further: Oh, I die for food! Here lie I down, and measure out my grave. Farewell, kind master!

Orl. Why, how now, Adam! no greater heart in thee? Live a little; comfort a little; cheer thyself a little. If this uncouth forest yield any thing savage, I will either be food for it, or bring it for food to thee. Thy conceit is nearer death than thy powers. For my sake be comfortable; hold death a while at the arm's end. I will be here with thee presently; and if I bring thee not something to eat, I will give thee leave to die: but if thou diest before I come, thou art a mocker of my labor. Well said! thou look'st cheerly: and I'll be with thee quickly.—Yet thou liest in the bleak air: Come, I will bear thee to some shelter; [*lifting him up*] and thou shalt not die for lack of a dinner, if there live anything in this desert. Cheerly, good Adam!

[*Bearing him away,* L., *scene changes.*

SCENE III:—*Another part of the Forest. A table set out. Enter* DUKE, AMIENS, *and* LORD, R.

Duke. (C.) I think he be transformed into a beast;
For I can nowhere find him like a man.

1*st Lord.* (R.) My lord, he is but even now gone hence;

Here was he merry, hearing of a song.

Duke. If he, compact of jars, grow musical,
We shall have shortly discord in the spheres:—
Go, seek him; tell him I would speak with him.

[*Enter* JAQUES, L.

1st Lord. He saves my labor by his own approach.

Duke. Why, how now, Monsieur! what a life is this,
That your poor friends must woo your company?
What! you look merrily.

Jaques. (L.) A Fool, a Fool!—I met a Fool i' th' forest,
A motley Fool—a miserable world!—
As I do live by food, I met a Fool
Who laid him down and basked him in the sun,
And railed on Lady Fortune in good terms,
In good set terms,—and yet a motley Fool.
"Good-morrow, Fool," quoth I: "No, sir," quoth he,
"Call me not Fool, till Heaven hath sent me fortune:"
And then he drew a dial from his poke,
And looking on it with lack-lustre eye,
Says, very wisely, "It is ten o'clock:
Thus we may see," quoth he, "how the world wags:
'T is but an hour ago since it was nine,
And after one hour more 't will be eleven;
And so, from hour to hour, we ripe and ripe,
And then, from hour to hour, we rot and rot;
And thereby hangs a tale." When I did hear
The motely Fool thus moral on the time,
My lungs began to crow like chanticleer.

That Fools should be so deep-contemplative;
And I did laugh, sans intermission,
An hour by his dial.—O noble Fool!
A worthy Fool! Motley's the only wear.

[*All retire to the table. Enter* ORLANDO, *with sword drawn*, L.

Orl. (L.) Forbear, and eat no more!

Jaques. Why, I have eat none yet.

Orl. Nor shalt not, till necessity be served.

Jaques. Of what kind should this cock come of?

Duke. [*Coming forward*] Art thou thus boldened, man, by thy distress?
Or else a rude despiser of good manners,
That in civility thou seem'st so empty?

Orl. You touched my vein at first; the thorny point
Of bare distress hath ta'en from me the show
Of smooth civility; yet am I inland bred,
And know some nurture. But forbear, I say:
He dies that touches any of this fruit,
Till I and my affairs are answered!

Duke. (R. C.) What would you have? Your gentleness shall force,
More than your force move us to gentleness.

Orl. I almost die for food, and let me have it.

Duke. Sit down and feed, and welcome to our table.

Orl. Speak you so gently? Pardon me, I pray you:
I thought that all things had been savage here;

And therefore put I on the countenance
Of stern commandment. But whate'er you are,
That in this desert inaccessible,
Under the shade of melancholy boughs,
Lose and neglect the creeping hours of time,
If ever you have looked on better days,
If ever been where bells have knolled to church,
If ever sat at any good man's feast,
If ever from your eyelids wiped a tear,
And know what 't is to pity and be pitied,
Let gentleness my strong enforcement be,—
In the which hope I blush and hide my sword.

Duke. True is it, that we have seen better days,
And have with holy bell been knolled to church,
And sat at good men's feasts, and wiped our eyes
Of drops that sacred pity hath engendered;
And therefore sit you down in gentleness,
And take upon command what help we have,
That to your wanting may be ministered.

Orl. Then, but forbear your food a little while,
Whiles, like a doe, I go to find my fawn
And give it food. There is an old poor man,
Who after me hath many a weary step
Limped in pure love; till he be first sufficed—
Oppressed with two weak evils, age and hunger—
I will not touch a bit.

Duke. Go, find him out,
And we will nothing waste till you return.

Orl. I thank ye; and be blessed for your good comfort! [*Exit*, L.

Duke. (C.) Thou see'st, we are not all alone unhappy;
This wide and universal theatre
Presents more woful pageants than the scene
Wherein we play in.

Jaques. (L. C.) All the world 's a stage,
And all the men and women merely players:
They have their exits and their entrances;
And one man in his time plays many parts,
His acts being seven ages. At first, the infant,
Mewling and puking in the nurse's arms.
And then, the whining school-boy, with his satchel
And shining morning face, creeping like snail
Unwillingly to school. And then, the lover,
Sighing like furnace, with a woful ballad
Made to his mistress' eyebrow. Then, a soldier,
Full of strange oaths, and bearded like the pard;
Jealous in honor, sudden and quick in quarrel,
Seeking the bubble reputation
Even in the cannon's mouth. And then, the justice,
In fair round belly, with good capon lined,
With eyes severe, and beard of formal cut,
Full of wise saws and modern instances,—
And so he plays his part. The sixth age shifts
Into the lean and slippered pantaloon,
With spectacles on nose and pouch on side;
His youthful hose, well saved, a world too wide
For his shrunk shank; and his big manly voice,
Turning again toward childish treble, pipes
And whistles in his sound. Last scene of all,

That ends this strange eventful history,
Is second childishness and mere oblivion;
Sans teeth, sans eyes, sans taste, sans—every thing.

[*All retire to table. Enter* ORLANDO *and* ADAM, L.

Duke. Welcome. Set down your venerable burden,
And let him feed.

Orl. I thank you most for him.

Adam. So had you need;
I scarce can speak to thank you for myself.

Duke. Welcome; fall to: I will not trouble you
As yet, to question you about your fortunes:—
Give us some music; and, good cousin, sing.

[AMIENS *advances*, C.

SONG.—*Amiens.*

Blow, blow, thou winter wind,
Thou art not so unkind
As man's ingratitude;
Thy tooth is not so keen,
Because thou art not seen,
Although thy breath be rude.

Heigh ho! sing, heigh ho! unto the green holly,
Most friendship is feigning, most loving mere folly—
Then, heigh ho, the holly!
This life is most jolly!

Freeze, freeze, thou bitter sky,
That dost not bite so nigh
As benefits forgot:

Though thou the waters warp
Thy sting is not so sharp
As friend remembered not.

Heigh ho! sing, heigh ho! unto the green holly,
Most friendship is feigning, most loving mere folly—
Then heigh ho, the holly!
This life is most jolly!

Duke. [*Comes forward*] If that you were the good Sir Rowland's son,—
As you have whispered faithfully you were,
And as mine eye doth his effigies witness,
Most truly limbed, and living in your face,—
Be truly welcome hither. I am the duke,
That loved your father. The residue of your fortune,
Go to my cave and tell me.—Good old man,
Thou art right welcome, as thy master is:—
Support him by the arm.—Give me your hand,
And let me all your fortunes understand.

Tableau. Curtain.

COSTUMES.

Duke.—Blue and white doublet and pantaloons; buff waistcoat; round green velvet hat and white plumes; russet boots; a vandyke, and gauntlets.

Amiens.—Blue doublet and pantaloons; white waistcoat; round purple hat and white plume; russet boots; vandyke, and gauntlets.

JAQUES.—Blue doublet and pantaloons, trimmed with brown fur; black hat and blue plume; russet boots; vandyke, and gauntlets.

ORLANDO.—Blue jacket; buff pantaloons; russet boots; vandyke, gauntlets; hat and plume; sword.

ADAM.—Attire of old man.

LORDS.—Foresters' costume of green, with gold lace.

REMARKS AND SUGGESTIONS.

These elegant scenes are very easy to perform, and to commit them to memory is to cultivate the taste and improve the heart. Such beautiful language one would not wish to forget. The amateur can not become too familiar with the masterpieces of Shakespeare. They are worth all the rest of English dramatic literature together.

Let the words of this drama be thoroughly studied, and frequently rehearsed before being rendered in public.

The costumes, properties, and attitudes, must be perfectly correct.

The *Prologue* at the beginning of the piece may be spoken by Amiens, by one of the lords, or by some good declaimer not cast in the play. It should be delivered in a loud, clear, and distinct tone, so as to attract the attention of the audience, and prepare their minds for the play.

Short musical interludes, between the scenes, add to the agreeable effect of the play.

NORVAL.

From Home's Douglas.

PERSONS REPRESENTED.

LORD RANDOLPH. LADY RANDOLPH.
NORVAL, *or* DOUGLAS. GLENALVON.
SERVANTS.

SCENE I:—*The Court of* LORD RANDOLPH'S *Castle. Enter* LADY RANDOLPH *hastily, accompanied by* LORD RANDOLPH *and* NORVAL, *with their swords drawn and bloody.*

Lady Rand. Not vain the stranger's fears! how fares my lord?

Lord Rand. That it fares well, thanks to this gallant youth,
Whose valor saved me from a wretched death!
As down the winding dale I walked alone,
At the cross-way four armed men attacked me:
Rovers, I judge, from the licentious camp,
Who would have quickly laid Lord Randolph low,
Had not this brave and generous stranger come,
Like my good angel, in the hour of fate,
And, mocking danger, made my foes his own.
They turned upon him, but his active arm
Struck to the ground, from whence they rose no more,
The fiercest two; the others fled amain,
And left him master of the bloody field.
Speak, Lady Randolph: upon beauty's tongue
Dwell accents pleasing to the brave and bold.
Speak, noble dame, and thank him for thy lord.

Lady Rand. My lord, I can not speak what now I feel.
My heart o'erflows with gratitude to Heaven
And to this noble youth, who, all unknown
To you and yours, deliberated not,
Nor paused at peril; but, humanely brave,
Fought on your side, against such fearful odds.
Have you yet learned of him, whom we should thank?
Whom call the savior of Lord Randolph's life?

Lord Rand. I asked that question, and he answered not: [*To the stranger.*
But I must know who my deliverer is.

Norval. A low-born man, of parentage obscure,
Who nought can boast but his desire to be
A soldier, and to gain a name in arms.

Lord Rand. Whoe'er thou art, thy spirit is ennobled
By the great King of kings! thou art ordained
And stamped a hero by the sovereign hand
Of nature! blush not, flower of modesty
As well as valor, to declare thy birth.

Norval. My name is Norval: on the Grampian hills
My father feeds his flocks; a frugal swain,
Whose constant cares were to increase his store,
And keep his only son, myself, at home.
For I had heard of battles, and I longed
To follow to the field some warlike lord:
And Heaven soon granted what my sire denied.
This moon, which rose last night, round as my shield,
Had not yet filled her horns, when, by her light,
A band of fierce barbarians, from the hills,
Rushed like a torrent down upon the vale,
Sweeping our flocks and herds. The shepherds fled
For safety and for succor. I alone,
With bended bow, and quiver full of arrows,
Hovered about the enemy, and marked
The road he took; then hasted to my friends,
Whom, with a troop of fifty chosen men,

I met advancing. The pursuit I led,
Till we o'ertook the spoil-encumbered foe.
We fought and conquered. Ere a sword was drawn,
An arrow from my bow had pierced their chief,
Who wore that day the arms which now I wear.
Returning home in triumph, I disdained
The shepherd's slothful life: and having heard
That our good king had summoned his bold peers
To lead their warriors to the Carron's side,
I left my father's house, and took with me
A chosen servant to conduct my steps;—
Yon trembling coward, who forsook his master.
Journeying with this intent, I passed these towers,
And, heaven-directed, came this day to do
The happy deed that gilds my humble name.

Lord Rand. He is as wise as brave. Was ever tale
With such a gallant modesty rehearsed?
My brave deliverer, thou shalt enter now
A nobler list, and in a monarch's sight,
Contend with princes for the prize of fame.
I will present thee to our Scottish king,
Whose valiant spirit ever valor loved.
Ah! my Matilda, wherefore starts that tear?

Lady Rand. I can not say: for various affections,
And strangely mingled, in my bosom swell;
Yet each of them may well command a tear.
I joy that thou art safe; and I admire
Him and his fortunes who hath wrought thy safety:
Yea, as my mind predicts, with thine his own.
Obscure and friendless, he the army sought,

Bent upon peril, in the range of death
Resolved to hunt for fame, and with his sword
To gain distinction which his birth denied.
In this attempt unknown he might have perished,
And gained, with all his valor, but oblivion.
Now graced by thee, his virtue serves no more
Beneath despair. The soldier now of hope
He stands conspicuous; fame and great renown
Are brought within the compass of his sword.
On this my mind reflected, whilst you spoke,
And blessed the wonder-working hand of Heaven.

Lord Rand. Pious and grateful ever are thy thoughts!
My deeds shall follow where thou point'st the way.
Next to myself, and equal to Glenalvon,
In honor and command shall Norval be.

Norval. I know not how to thank you. Rude I am
In speech and manners; never till this hour
Stood I in such a presence: yet, my lord,
There 's something in my breast which makes me bold
To say, that Norval ne'er will shame thy favor.

Lady Rand. I will be sworn thou wilt not. Thou shalt be
My knight; and ever, as thou did'st to-day,
With happy valor guard the life of Randolph.

Lord Rand. Well hast thou spoke. Let me forbid reply. [*To* NORVAL.
We are thy debtors still; thy high desert

O'ertops our gratitude. I must proceed,
As was at first intended, to the camp.
Some of my train, I see, are speeding hither,
Impatient, doubtless, of their lord's delay.
Go with me, Norval, and thine eyes shall see
The chosen warriors of thy native land,
Who languish for the fight, and beat the air
With brandished swords.

Norval. Let us begone, my lord.

Lord Rand. [*To* LADY RANDOLPH] About the time that the declining sun
Shall his broad orbit o'er yon hills suspend,
Expect us to return. This night once more
Within these walls I rest; my tent I pitch
To-morrow in the field. Prepare the feast.
Free is his heart who for his country fights;
He in the eve of battle may resign
Himself to social pleasure; sweetest then,
When danger to a soldier's soul endears
The human joy that never may return.

[*Exeunt* LORD RANDOLPH *and* NORVAL.

Lady Rand. His parting words have struck a fatal truth.
O Douglas! Douglas! tender was the time
When we two parted, ne'er to meet again!
How many years of anguish and despair
Has heaven annexed to those swift-passing hours
Of love and fondness!
At every happy parent I repine!
How blest the mother of young gallant Norval!

She for a living husband bore her pains,
And heard him bless her when a man was born:
She nursed her smiling infant on her breast;
Tended the child, and reared the pleasing boy:
She, with affection's triumph, saw the youth
In grace and comeliness surpass his peers:
Whilst I to a dead husband bore a son,
And to the roaring waters gave my child.
I thought, that, had the son of Douglas lived,
He might have been like this young gallant stranger,
And paired with him in features and in shape;
In all endowments, as in years, I deem,
My boy with blooming Norval might have numbered.
Whilst thus I mused, a spark from fancy fell
On my sad heart, and kindled up a fondness
For this young stranger, wand'ring from his home,
And like an orphan cast upon my care.

SCENE II:—*The same. Enter* LADY RANDOLPH, *excitedly.*

Lady Rand. 'T is he! 't is he himself! It is my son!
O sovereign mercy! 'T was my child I saw!
Unparalleled event!
Reaching from heaven to earth, Jehovah's arm
Snatched from the waves, and brings to me my son!
Judge of the widow and the orphan's father!
Accept a widow's and a mother's thanks
For such a gift!

How soon he gazed on bright and burning arms,
Spurned the low dunghill where his fate had thrown
him,
And towered up to the region of his sire!
How fondly did my eyes devour the boy.
Mysterious nature, with the unseen cord
Of powerful instinct, drew me to my own.
But now I long to see his face again,
Examine every feature, and find out
The lineaments of Douglas, or my own.
But, most of all, I long to let him know
Who his true parents are, to clasp his neck,
And tell him all the story of his father.
'Be still, my heart, he comes, my Douglas comes!'

[*Enter* NORVAL.

The soldier's loftiness, the pride and pomp
Investing awful war, Norval, I see,
Transport thy youthful mind.

Norval. Ah! should they not?
Blest be the hour I left my father's house!
I might have been a shepherd all my days,
And stole obscurely to a peasant's grave.
Now, if I live, with mighty chiefs I stand;
And, if I fall, with noble dust I lie.

Lady Rand. There is a gen'rous spirit in thy
breast
That could have well sustained a prouder fortune.
Since lucky chance has left us here alone,
Unseen, unheard, by human eye or ear,
I will amaze thee with a wond'rous tale.

Norval. Let there be danger, lady, with the secret,
That I may hug it to my grateful heart,
And prove my faith. Command my sword, my life:
These are the sole possessions of poor Norval.

Lady Rand. Know'st thou these gems?

[*She holds up sparkling jewels.*

Norval. Durst I believe mine eyes,
I 'd say I knew them, and they were my father's.

Lady Rand. Thy father's, say'st thou! ah! they were thy father's!

Norval. I saw them once, and curiously inquired
Of both my parents, whence such splendor came?
But I was checked, and more could never learn.

Lady Rand. Then learn of me, thou art not Norval's son.

Norval. Not Norval's son!

Lady Rand. Nor of a shepherd sprung.

Norval. Lady, who am I, then?

Lady Rand. Noble thou art;
For noble was thy sire!

Norval. I will believe—
O! tell me farther! Say, who was my father?

Lady Rand. Douglas!

Norval. Lord Douglas, whom to-day I saw?

Lady Rand. His younger brother.

Norval. And in yonder camp?

Lady Rand. Alas!

Norval. You make me tremble—Sighs and tears!
Lives my brave father?

Lady Rand. Ah! too brave indeed!

He fell in battle ere thyself was born.

Norval. Ah me, unhappy! ere I saw the light?
But does my mother live? I may conclude,
From my own fate, her portion has been sorrow.

Lady Rand. She lives; but wastes her life in constant woe,
Weeping her husband slain, her infant lost.

Norval. You that are skilled in the sad story
Of my unhappy parents, and with tears
Bewail their destiny, now have compassion
Upon the offspring of the friends you loved!
O tell me who, and where my mother is!
Oppressed by a base world, perhaps she bends
Beneath the weight of other ills than grief;
And, desolate, implores of Heaven the aid
Her son should give. It is, it must be so—
Your countenance confesses that she 's wretched.
O tell me her condition! Can the sword—
Who shall resist me in a parent's cause?

Lady Rand. Thy virtue ends her woe! My son! my son!

Norval. Art thou my mother?

Lady Rand. I am thy mother, and the wife of Douglas. [*Falls upon his neck.*

Norval. O heaven and earth, how wondrous is my fate!
Art thou my mother! Ever let me kneel!

Lady Rand. Image of Douglas! Fruit of fatal love!
All that I owe thy sire, I pay to thee.

Norval. Respect and admiration still possess me,
Checking the love and fondness of a son.
Yet I was filial to my humble parents.
But did my sire surpass the rest of men,
As thou excellest all of womankind?

Lady Rand. Arise, my son! In me thou dost behold
The poor remains of beauty once admired:
The autumn of my days is come already;
For sorrow made my summer haste away.
Yet in my prime I equaled not thy father:
His eyes were like the eagle's, yet sometimes
Liker the dove's; and, as he pleased, he won
All hearts with softness, or with spirit awed.

Norval. How did he fall? Sure 't was a bloody field
When Douglas died. O, I have much to ask!

Lady Rand. Hereafter thou shalt hear the lengthened tale
Of all thy father's and thy mother's woes.
At present this: thou art the rightful heir
Of yonder castle, and the wide domains
Which now Lord Randolph, as my husband, holds.
But thou shalt not be wronged; I have the power
To right thee still; before the king I'll kneel,
And call Lord Douglas to protect his blood.

Norval. The blood of Douglas will protect itself.

Lady Rand. But we shall need both friends and favor, boy,
To wrest thy lands and lordship from the gripe

Of Randolph and his kinsman. Yet I think
My tale will move each gentle heart to pity;
My life incline the virtuous to believe.

Norval. To be the son of Douglas is to me
Inheritance enough. Declare my birth,
And in the field I 'll seek for fame and fortune.

Lady Rand. Thou dost not know what perils and injustice
Await the poor man's valor. O! my son!
The noblest blood of all the land 's abashed,
Having no lackey but pale poverty.
Too long hast thou been thus attended, Douglas!
Too long hast thou been deemed a peasant's child.
The wanton heir of some inglorious chief
Perhaps has scorned thee, in the youthful sports;
Whilst thy indignant spirit swelled in vain.
Such contumely thou no more shalt bear:
But how I purpose to redress thy wrongs
Must be hereafter told. Prudence directs
That we should part before yon chiefs return.
Retire, and from thy rustic follower's hand
Receive a billet, which thy mother's care,
Anxious to see thee, dictated before
This casual opportunity arose
Of private conference. Its purport mark;
For, as I there appoint, we meet again.
Leave me, my son, and frame thy manners still
To Norval's, not to noble Douglas' state.

Norval. I will remember. Where is Norval now?
That good old man!

Lady Rand. At hand, concealed he lies,
A useful witness. But beware, my son,
Of yon Glenalvon; in his guilty breast
Resides a villain's shrewdness, ever prone
To false conjecture. He hath grieved my heart.

Norval. Has he, indeed? Then, let yon false Glenalvon
Beware of me. [*Exit.*

Lady Rand. There burst the smothered flame!
O thou all-righteous and eternal King!
Who Father of the fatherless art called,
Protect my son!—Thy inspiration, Lord,
Hath filled his bosom with that sacred fire,
Which in the breasts of his forefathers burned:
Set him on high, like them, that he may shine
The star and glory of his native land!
Then let the minister of death descend,
And bear my willing spirit to its place.
Yonder they come. How do bad women find
Unchanging aspects to conceal their guilt?
When I, by reason, and by justice urged,
Full hardly can dissemble with these men
In nature's pious cause.

[*Enter* LORD RANDOLPH *and* GLENALVON.

Lord Rand. Yon gallant chief,
Of arms enamored, all repose disclaims.

Lady Rand. Be not, my lord, by his example swayed:
Arrange the business of to-morrow now,
And, when you enter, speak of war no more. [*Exit.*

Lord Rand. 'T is so, by heaven! her mien, her voice, her eye,
And her impatience to be gone, confirm it.
Glen. He parted from her now: behind the mount,
Amongst the trees, I saw him glide along.
Lord Rand. For sad, sequestered virtue she 's renowned!
Glen. Most true, my lord.
Lord Rand. Yet this distinguished dame
Invites a youth, the acquaintance of a day,
Alone to meet her at the midnight hour.
This assignation [*shows a letter*] the assassin freed,
Her manifest affection for the youth,
Might breed suspicion in a husband's brain,
Whose gentle consort all for love had wedded;
Much more in mine. Matilda never loved me.
Let no man, after me, a woman wed,
Whose heart he knows he has not; tho' she brings
A mine of gold, a kingdom for her dowry,
For let her seem, like the night's shadowy queen,
Cold and contemplative;—he can not trust her:
She may, she will, bring shame and sorrow on him;
The worst of sorrows, and the worst of shames!
Glen. Yield not, my lord, to such afflicting thoughts,
But let the spirit of a husband sleep,
Till your own senses make a sure conclusion.
This billet must to blooming Norval go:
At the next turn awaits my trusty spy;
I 'll give it him, refitted for his master

In the close thicket take your secret stand;
The moon shines bright, and your own eyes may judge
Of their behavior.

Lord Rand. Thou dost counsel well.

Glen. Permit me now to make one slight essay.
Of all the trophies which vain mortals boast,
By wit, by valor, or by wisdom won,
The first and fairest in a young man's eye,
Is woman's captive heart. Successful love
With glorious fumes intoxicates the mind!
And the proud conqueror in triumph moves
Air-born, exalted above vulgar men.

Lord Rand. And what avails this maxim?

Glen. Much, my lord.
Withdraw a little: I'll accost young Norval,
And with ironical derisive counsel
Explore his spirit. If he is no more
Than humble Norval, by thy favor raised,
Brave as he is, he'll shrink astonished from me:
But if he be the favorite of the fair,
Loved by the first of Caledonia's dames,
He'll turn upon me, as the lion turns
Upon the hunter's spear.

Lord Rand. 'T is shrewdly thought.

Glen. When we grow loud, draw near. But let my lord
His rising wrath restrain. [*Exit* RANDOLPH.
'T is strange, by heaven!
That she should run full tilt her fond career,

To one so little known. She, too, that seemed
Pure as the winter stream, when ice, embossed,
Whitens its course. Even I did think her chaste,
Whose charity exceeds not. Precious sex,
Whose deeds lascivious pass Glenalvon's thoughts!
[NORVAL *appears.*
His port I love; he 's in a proper mood
To chide the thunder, if at him it roared.
Has Norval seen the troops?
Norval. The setting sun,
With yellow radiance lightened all the vale;
And as the warriors moved, each polished helm,
Corslet, or spear, glanced back his gilded beams.
The hill they climbed, and halting at its top,
Of more than mortal size, towering, they seemed,
A host angelic, clad in burning arms.
Glen. Thou talk'st it well; no leader of our host,
In sounds more lofty, speaks of glorious war.
Norval. If I shall e'er acquire a leader's name,
My speech will be less ardent. Novelty
Now prompts my tongue, and youthful admiration
Vents itself freely; since no part is mine
Of praise pertaining to the great in arms.
Glen. You wrong yourself, brave sir; your martial deeds
Have ranked you with the great. But mark me, Norval;
Lord Randolph's favor now exalts your youth
Above his veterans of famous service.
Let me, who know the soldiers, counsel you.

Give them all honor; seem not to command:
Else they will scarcely brook your late sprung power,
Which nor alliance props, nor birth adorns.
Norval. Sir, I have been accustomed all my days
To hear and speak the plain and simple truth:
And though I have been told, that there are men
Who borrow friendship's tongue to speak their scorn,
Yet in such language I am little skilled
Therefore I thank Glenalvon for his counsel,
Although it sounded harshly. Why remind
Me of my birth obscure? Why slur my power
With such contemptuous terms?
Glen. I did not mean
To gall your pride, which now I see is great.
Norval. My pride!
Glen. Suppress it as you wish to prosper.
Your pride 's excessive. Yet for Randolph's sake
I will not leave you to its rash direction.
If thus you swell, and frown at high-born men,
Think you they will endure a shepherd's scorn?
Norval. A shepherd's scorn!
Glen. Yes; if you presume
To bend on soldiers these disdainful eyes,
What will become of you?
Norval. If this were told— [*Aside.*
Hast thou no fears for thy presumptuous self?
Glen. Ha! dost thou threaten me?
Norval. Did'st thou not hear?
Glen. Unwillingly I did; a nobler foe
Had not been questioned thus. But such as thee—

Norval. Whom dost thou think me?
Glen. Norval.
Norval. So I am—
And who is Norval in Glenalvon's eyes?
Glen. A peasant's son, a wand'ring beggar-boy,
At best no more, even if he speaks the truth.
Norval. False as thou art, dost thou suspect my truth?
Glen. Thy truth! thou 'rt all a lie; and false as hell
Is the vain-glorious tale thou told'st to Randolph.
Nor. If I were chained, unarmed, and bedrid old,
Perhaps I should revile: but as I am
I have no tongue to rail. The humble Norval
Is of a race who strive not but with deeds.
Did I not fear to freeze thy shallow valor,
And make thee sink too soon beneath my sword,
I 'd tell thee—what thou art. I know thee well.
Glen. Dost thou not know Glenalvon, born to command
Ten thousand slaves like thee—
Norval. Villain, no more!
Draw and defend thy life. I did design
To have defied thee in another cause:
But Heaven accelerates its vengeance on thee.
Now for my own and Lady Randolph's wrongs.
[*Enter* LORD RANDOLPH.
Lord Rand. Hold, I command you both. The man that stirs
Makes me his foe.

Norval. Another voice than thine
That threat had vainly sounded, noble Randolph.
Glen. Hear him, my lord; he 's wond'rous condescending!
Mark the humility of shepherd Norval!
Norval. Now you may scoff in safety.
[*Sheathes his sword.*
Lord Rand. Speak not thus,
Taunting each other; but unfold to me
The cause of quarrel, then I judge betwixt you.
Norval. Nay, my good lord, though I revere you much,
My cause I plead not, nor demand your judgment.
I blush to speak; I will not, can not speak
The opprobrious words that I from him have borne.
To the liege-lord of my dear native land
I owe a subject's homage; but even him
And his high arbitration I 'd reject.
Within my bosom reigns another lord;
Honor, sole judge and umpire of itself.
If my free speech offend you, noble Randolph,
Revoke your favors, and let Norval go
Hence as he came, alone, but not dishonored.
Lord Rand. Thus far I 'll mediate with impartial voice:
The ancient foe of Caledonia's land
Now waves his banners o'er her frighted fields.
Suspend your purpose, till your country's arms
Repel the bold invader; then decide
The private quarrel.

Glen. I agree to this.

Norval. And I. [*Enter* SERVANT.

Servant. The banquet waits.

Lord Rand. We come.

[*Exit* RANDOLPH *and* SERVANT.

Glen. Norval,
Let not our variance mar the social hour,
Nor wrong the hospitality of Randolph.
Nor frowning anger, nor yet wrinkled hate,
Shall stain my countenance. Smooth thou thy brow;
Nor let our strife disturb the gentle dame.

Norval. Think not so lightly, sir, of my resentment;
When we contend again, our strife is mortal.

[*Exeunt.*

COSTUME.

FOR an idea of correct costume, for the male characters, see illustration on page 128. Lady Randolph should wear a long robe dress, gathered round the waist, and fastened with a belt of leather and silver, mixed like a chain. Over this a long mantle, embroidered, and fastened by a brooch on the breast. She may also wear a necklace and bracelets.

MATRIMONIAL INFELICITIES.

From Sheridan's School for Scandal.

PERSONS REPRESENTED.

LADY TEAZLE. SIR PETER TEAZLE.

SCENE:—*A Room in* SIR PETER'S *House. Enter* LADY TEAZLE *and* SIR PETER, L.

Sir Peter. Lady Teazle, Lady Teazle, I 'll not bear it!

Lady T. (R.) Sir Peter, Sir Peter, you may bear it or not, as you please; but I ought to have my own way in every thing; and, what 's more, I will, too. What! though I was educated in the country, I know very well that women of fashion in London are accountable to nobody after they are married.

Sir P. Very well, ma'am, very well—so a husband is to have no influence, no authority?

Lady T. Authority! No, to be sure:—if you wanted authority over me, you should have adopted me, and not married me: I am sure you were old enough.

Sir P. Old enough! ay—there it is. Well, well, Lady Teazle, though my life may be made unhappy by your temper, I 'll not be ruined by your extravagance.

Lady T. My extravagance! I 'm sure I 'm not more extravagant than a woman of fashion ought to be.

Sir P. No, no, madam, you shall throw away no more sums on such unmeaning luxury. Why, you spend as much to furnish your dressing-room with flowers in winter as would suffice to turn the Pantheon into a green-house, and give a *fête champêtre* at Christmas.

Lady T. And, am I to blame, Sir Peter, because flowers are dear in cold weather? You should find fault with the climate, and not with me. For my part, I 'm sure, I wish it was spring all the year round, and that roses grew under our feet.

Sir P. Oons! Madam—if you had been born to this, I should n't wonder at your talking thus; but you forget what your situation was when I married you.

Lady T. No, no. I do n't; 't was a very disagreeable one, or I should never have married you.

Sir P. Yes, yes, madam, you were then in somewhat a humbler style:—the daughter of a plain country squire. Recollect, Lady Teazle, when I saw you first, sitting at your tambour, in a pretty figured linen gown, with a bunch of keys at your side; your hair combed smooth over a roll, and your apartment hung round with fruits in worsted of your own working.

Lady T. O yes! I remember it very well, and a curious life I led.—My daily occupation to inspect the dairy, superintend the poultry, make extracts from the family receipt-book,—and comb my aunt Deborah's lap-dog.

Sir P. Yes, yes, ma'am, 't was so indeed.

Lady T. And then, you know, my evening amusements! To draw patterns for ruffles, which I had not materials to make up; to play Pope Joan with the curate; to read a sermon to my aunt; or to be stuck down to an old spinet to strum my father to sleep after a fox-chase. [*Crosses,* L.

Sir P. (R.) I am glad you have so good a memory.—Yes, madam, these were the recreations I took you from; but now you must have your coach—*vis-à-vis*—and three powdered footmen before your chair; and, in the summer, a pair of white cats to draw you to Kensington gardens. No recollection, I suppose, when you were content to ride double, behind the butler, on a docked coach-horse.

Lady T. (L.) No—I declare I never did that: I deny the butler and the coach-horse.

Sir P. This, madam, was your situation; and what have I done for you? I have made you a woman of fashion, of fortune, of rank—in short, I have made you my wife.

Lady T. Well, then,—and there is but one thing more you can make me to add to the obligation, that is—

Sir P. My widow, I suppose?

Lady T. Hem! hem!

Sir P. I thank you, madam—but do n't flatter yourself; for though your ill-conduct may disturb my peace of mind, it shall never break my heart, I promise you: however, I am equally obliged to you for the hint. [*Crosses*, L.

Lady T. Then why will you endeavor to make yourself so disagreeable to me, and thwart me in every little elegant expense?

Sir P. (L.) 'Slife, madam, I say, had you any of these little elegant expenses when you married me?

Lady T. Lud, Sir Peter! would you have me be out of the fashion?

Sir P. The fashion, indeed! What had you to do with the fashion before you married me?

Lady T. For my part, I should think you would like to have your wife thought a woman of taste.

Sir P. Ay—there again—taste! Zounds! madam, you had no taste when you married me!

Lady T. That 's very true, indeed, Sir Peter! and, after having married you, I should never pretend to taste again, I allow. But now, Sir Peter, since we have finished our daily jangle, I presume I may go to my engagement at Lady Sneerwell's.

Sir P. Ay, there 's another precious circumstance—a charming set of acquaintance you have made there.

Lady T. Nay, Sir Peter, they are all people of rank and fortune, and remarkably tenacious of reputation.

Sir P. Yes, egad, they are tenacious of reputation with a vengeance; for they do n't choose any body should have a character but themselves!—Such a crew! Ah! many a wretch has rid on a hurdle who has done less mischief than these utterers of forged tales, coiners of scandal, and clippers of reputation.

Lady T. What! would you restrain the freedom of speech?

Sir P. Ah! they have made you just as bad as any one of the society.

Lady T. Why, I believe I do bear a part with a tolerable grace.

Sir P. Grace, indeed!

Lady T. But I vow I bear no malice against the people I abuse. When I say an ill-natured thing, 't is out of pure good humor; and, I take it for granted, they deal exactly in the same manner with me. But, Sir Peter, you know you promised to come to Lady Sneerwell's too.

Sir P. Well, well, I'll call in just to look after my own character.

Lady T. Then, indeed, you must make haste after me, or you 'll be too late. So, good bye to ye.

[*Exit* Lady Teazle, r.

Sir P. So—I have gained much by my intended expostulation: yet, with what a charming air she contradicts every thing I say, and how pleasantly she shows her contempt for my authority! Well, though I can't make her love me, there is great satisfaction in quarrelling with her; and I think she never appears to such advantage as when she is doing every thing in her power to plague me.

[*Exit*, L.

COSTUMES.

SIR PETER.—Drab or salmon-colored velvet coat and breeches, trimmed with silver; white satin vest; white silk stockings; shoes; buckles; lace ruffles; etc.

LADY TEAZLE.—Elegant white gauze dress, handsomely worked with silver flowers; white satin petticoat and body; and plume of feathers.

COUNTRY VERSUS CITY.

From The Hunchback by Knowles.

PERSONS REPRESENTED.

FATHOM, *a country servant.* THOMAS, *a city servant.*

SCENE:—*An Apartment in a City House. Enter* THOMAS *and* FATHOM, R.

Thomas. Well, Fathom, is thy mistress up?

Fathom. She is, Master Thomas, and breakfasted.

Thomas. She stands it well! 'T was five, you say, when she came home; and now it wants three-quarters of an hour of ten! Wait till her stock of country health is out.

Fathom. 'T will come to that, Master Thomas, before she lives another month in town! Three, four, five, six o'clock, are now the hours she keeps. 'T was otherwise with her in the country. There my mistress used to rise what time she now lies down.

Thomas. Why, yes; she's changed since she came hither.

Fathom. Changed, do you say, Master Thomas? Changed, forsooth! I know not the thing in which she is not changed, saving that she is still a woman.

I tell thee there is no keeping pace with her moods. In the country she had none of them. When I brought what she asked for, it was "thank you, Fathom," and no more to do; but now, nothing contents her. Hark ye! were you a gentleman, Master Thomas,—for then you know you would be a different kind of a man,—how many times would you have your coat altered?

Thomas. Why, Master Fathom, as many times as it would take to make it fit me.

Fathom. Good! But supposing it fitted thee at the first?

Thomas. Then would I not have it altered at all.

Fathom. Good! Thou would'st be a reasonable gentleman. Thou would'st have a conscience. Now hark to a tale about my lady's last gown. How many times, think you, took I it back to the sempstress?

Thomas. Thrice, may be.

Fathom. Thrice, may be! Twenty times, may be; and not a turn too many for the truth on 't. Twenty times, on the oath of the sempstress. Now, mark me—can you count?

Thomas. After a fashion.

Fathom. You have much to be thankful for, Master Thomas; you city serving-men know a world of things, which we in the country never dream of. Now mark:—four times took I it back for the flounce; twice for the sleeves; thrice for the tucker. How many times in all is that?

Thom. Eight times, to a fraction, Master Fathom.

Fathom. What a master of figures you are! Eight times—now recollect that! And then found she fault with the trimmings. Now, tell me how many times took I back the gown for the trimmings?

Thomas. Eight times more, perhaps!

Fathom. Ten times to a certainty. How many times makes that?

Thomas. Eighteen, Master Fathom, by the rule of addition.

Fathom. And how many times more will make twenty?

Thomas. Twice, by the same rule.

Fathom. Thou hast worked with thy pencil and slate, Master Thomas! Well, ten times, as I said, took I back the gown for the trimmings: and was she content after all? I warrant you no, or my ears did not pay for it. She wished, she said, that the slattern sempstress had not touched the gown; for naught had she done, but botched it. Now what, think you, had the sempstress done to the gown?

Thomas. To surmise that, I must be learned in the sempstress's art.

Fathom. The sempstress's art! Thou has hit it! Oh, the sweet sempstress! The excellent sempstress! Mistress of her scissors and needles, which are pointless and edgeless to her art! The sempstress had done nothing to the gown, yet raves and storms my mistress at her for having botched it in the making and altering; and orders her straight to make another one, which home the sempstress brings on Tuesday last.

Thomas. And found thy fair mistress as many faults with that?

Fathom. Not one! She finds it a very pattern of a gown! A well-setting flounce! The sleeves a fit—the tucker a fit—the trimmings her fancy to a T—ha! ha! ha! and she praises the sempstress—ha! ha! ha! and she smiles at me, and I smile—ha! ha! ha! and the sempstress smiles—ha! ha! ha! Now, why did the sempstress smile?

Thomas. That she had succeeded so well in her art.

Fathom. Thou hast hit it again. The jade must have been born a sempstress. If ever I marry, she shall work for my wife. The gown was the same gown, and there was my mistress's twentieth mood!

Thomas. What, think you, will Master Walter say when he comes back? I fear he'll hardly know his country maid again. Has she yet fixed her wedding-day?

Fathom. She has, Master Thomas. I coaxed it from her maid. She marries Monday week.

Thomas. Comes not Master Walter back to-day?

Fathom. Your master expects him. [*Bell ringing*, L.] Perhaps that's he. I pr'ythee go and open the door; do, Master Thomas, do; for proves it my master, he'll surely question me.

Thomas. And what should I do?

Fathom. Answer him, Master Thomas, and make

him none the wiser. He'll go mad, when he learns how my lady flaunts it! Go, open the door, I pr'ythee. Fifty things, Master Thomas, know you, for one thing that I know; you can turn and twist a matter into any other kind of matter, and then twist and turn it back again, if needs be; so much you servants of the town beat us of the country, Master Thomas. Open the door, now; do, Master Thomas, do! [*Exeunt*, L.

COSTUMES.

FATHOM.—Green jacket, ornamented; buff breeches; white stockings, and shoes.

THOMAS.—Plain blue coat; yellow waistcoat and breeches; brown stockings; black shoes.

THE WITTY SERVANT.

From Shakespeare's Two Gentlemen of Verona.

PERSONS REPRESENTED.

VALENTINE, *a gentleman of Verona.* SPEED, *his servant.*

SCENE:—*A Room. Enter* VALENTINE, SPEED *following, with a lady's glove in his hand.*

Speed. (R.) Sir, your glove.

Val. (L.) Not mine; my gloves are on.

Speed. Why, then, this may be yours, for this is but one.

Val. Ha! let me see. [*Crosses to him*] Ay, give it me, it's mine.—Sweet ornament, that decks a thing divine! [*Kisses it*] Ah, Silvia! Silvia!

Speed. Madam Silvia! Madam Silvia!

[*At stairs*, L.

Val. (R.) How now, sirrah!

Speed. She is not within hearing, sir.

Val. Why, sir, who bade you call her?

Speed. Your worship, sir; or else I mistook.

Val. Well, you'll still be too forward.

[*Crosses*, L.

Speed. And yet I was last chidden for being too slow. [*Goes down*, R.

Val. Go to, sir. Tell me, do you know Madam Silvia?

Speed. She that your worship loves?

Val. Why, how know you that I am in love?

Speed. Marry, by these special marks. First, you have learned, like Sir Proteus, to wreath your arms like a malcontent; to relish a love song, like a robin-redbreast; to walk alone, like one that had the pestilence; to sigh, like a schoolboy that had lost his A, B, C; to weep, like a young wench that had buried her grandam; to fast, like one that takes diet; to watch, like one that fears robbing; to speak puling, like a beggar at Hallowmas. You were wont, when you laughed, to crow like a cock; when you walked, to walk like one of the lions; when you fasted, it was presently after dinner; when you looked sadly, it was for want of money; and now you are metamorphosed with a mistress, that, when I look on you, I can hardly think you are my master.

Val. Are all these things perceived in me?

[*Crosses*, R.

Speed. They are all perceived without ye.

Val. Without me? they can not.

Speed. Without you? nay, that's certain; you are so without these follies, that these follies are within you.

Val. But, tell me, dost thou know my lady Silvia?

Speed. She that you gaze on so, as she sits at supper?

Val. Hast thou observed that? Even she, I mean.

Speed. Why, sir, I know her not.

Val. Dost thou know her by my gazing on her, and yet knowest her not?

Speed. Is she not hard-favored, sir?

Val. Not so fair, boy, as well-favored.

Speed. Sir, I know that well enough.

Val. What dost thou know?

Speed. That she is not so fair, as (of you) well-favored.

Val. I mean, that her beauty is exquisite, but her favor infinite.

Speed. That's because the one is painted, and the other out of all count.

Val. How painted? and how out of count?

Speed. Marry, sir, so painted to make her fair, that no man counts of her beauty.

Val. How esteemest thou me? I account of her beauty.

Speed. You never saw her since she was deformed.

Val. How long hath she been deformed?

Speed. Ever since you loved her.

Val. I have loved her ever since I saw her; and still I see her beautiful. [*Crosses*, L.

Speed. If you love her, you can not see her.

Val. Why?

Speed. Because love is blind. Oh, that you had mine eyes, or your own had the lights they were wont to have, when you chid at Sir Proteus for going ungartered.

Val. What should I see then?

Speed. Your own present folly; and her passing deformity; for he, being in love, could not see to garter his hose; and you, being in love, can not see to put on your hose.

Val. [*Crosses*, R.] Belike, boy, then, you are in love; for last morning you could not see to wipe my shoes.

Speed. True, sir; I was in love with my bed. I thank you, you swinged me for my love, which makes me bolder to chide you for yours. [*Exeunt.*

COSTUMES.

VALENTINE.—Green velvet shirt, with hanging sleeves lined with white satin, and richly embroidered with gold; white satin and gold tight under-sleeves and pouch; white silk pantaloons; black velvet shoes, with strap on the instep; black velvet hat, and white feather.

SPEED.—Green and black flowered close-fitting woolen suit; green stockings, and puffs.

QUACKERY DISCOVERED.

From the Honeymoon, by John Tobin.

PERSONS REPRESENTED.

LAMPEDO. HOSTESS. VOLANTE. BALTHAZAR.

SCENE I:—*An Inn. Enter* BALTHAZAR, *as having fallen from his horse, supported by* VOLANTE, *and preceded by the* HOSTESS, L.

Hostess. This way, this way, if you please.—Alas, poor gentleman! [*Brings a chair*] How do you feel now, sir? [*They set him down.*

Bal. I almost think my brains are where they should be—
Confound the jade!—Though they dance merrily
To their own music.

Vol. Is the surgeon sent for?

Hostess. Here he comes. [*Enter* LAMPEDO, L.

Lam. Is this the gentleman?

[*Advances toward* BALTHAZAR.

Bal. I want no surgeon; all my bones are whole.

Vol. Pray take advice!

Bal. Well!—doctor, I have doubts
Whether my soul be shaken from my body,—
Else I am whole.

Lam. Then you are safe, depend on 't;
Your soul and body are not yet divorced—
Though if they were, we have a remedy.
Nor have you fracture, sir, simple or compound:
Yet very feverish! I begin to fear
Some inward bruise—a very raging pulse!—
We must phlebotomize!

Bal. You won't! Already
There is too little blood in these old veins
To do my cause full justice.

Lam. Quick, and feverish!—
He must lie down a little; for as yet
His blood and spirits being all in motion,
There is too great confusion in the symptoms,
To judge discreetly from.

Bal. I'll not lie down!

Vol. Nay, for an hour or so?

Bal. Well, be it so.

Hostess. I'll show you to a chamber: this way, this way, if you please. [*Exeunt all but* LAMPEDO, R.

Lam. 'T is the first patient, save the miller's mare,
And an old lady's cat, that has the phthisic,
That I have touched these six weeks.—Well, good hostess, [*Re-enter* HOSTESS, R.
How fares your guest?

Hostess. He must not go to-night!

Lam. No; nor to-morrow—

Hostess. Nor the next day, neither!

Lam. Leave that to me.—

Hostess. He has no hurt, I fear?

Lam. None:—but, as you are his cook, and I'm his doctor.
Such things may happen.—You must make him ill.
And I must keep him so—for, to say truth,
'T is the first biped customer I've handled
This many a day: they fall but slowly in—
Like the subscribers to my work on fevers.

Hostess. Hard times, indeed!—No business stirring my way.

Lam. So I should guess, from your appearance, hostess.
You look as if, for lack of company,
You were obliged to eat up your whole larder.

Hostess. Alas! 'T is so—
Yet I contrive to keep my spirits up.

Lam. Yes: and your flesh too.—Look at me.

Hostess. Why, truly,

You look half starved.

Lam. Half starved! I wish you 'd tell me
Which half of me is fed. I show more points
Than an old horse that has been three weeks
pounded—
Yet I do all to tempt them into sickness.
Have I not in the jaws of bankruptcy,
And to the desolation of my person,
Painted my shop, that it looks like a rainbow?
New double-gilt my pestle and my mortar,
That some, at a distance, take it for the sun?
And blazed in flaming letters o'er my door,
Each one a glorious constellation,
"Surgeon, Apothecary, Accoucher"—
(For midwife is grown vulgar)?—Yet they ail not.
Phials and gallipots still keep their ranks,
As if there was no cordial virtue in them.
The healing chime of pulverizing drugs
They shun as 't were a tolling bell, or death-watch.
I never give a dose, or set a limb!
But, come, we must devise, we must devise,
How to make much of this same guest, sweet hostess.

Hostess. You know I always make the most of
them.

Lam. Spoke like an ancient tapstress!—Come,
let's in—
And, whilst I soothe my bowels with an omelette,
(For like a nest of new-waked rooklings, hostess,
They caw for provender,) and take a glass
Of thy Falernian—we will think of means—

For though to cure men be beyond our skill,
'T is hard, indeed, if we can't keep them ill.

[*Exeunt*, R.

SCENE II:—*The Inn.* *Enter* LAMPEDO 1*st; and* HOSTESS 2*d*, R.

Hostess. Nay, nay, another fortnight.

Lam. It can't be.
The man 's as well as I am:—have some mercy!—
He hath been here almost three weeks already.

Hostess. Well, then, a week.

Lam. We may detain him a week.

[*Enter* BALTHAZAR *behind from door in flat*, R., *in his night-gown, with a drawn sword.*

You talk now like a reasonable hostess,
That sometimes has a reckoning—with her conscience.

Hostess. He still believes he has an inward bruise.

Lam. I would to Heaven he had! Or that he 'd slipt
His shoulder-blade, or broke a leg or two,
(Not that I bear his person any malice)
Or luxed an arm, or even sprained his ankle!

Hostess. Ay, broken any thing except his neck.

Lam. However, for a week I 'll manage him,
Though he has the constitution of a horse—
A farrier should prescribe for him!

Bal. A farrier! [*Aside.*

Lam. To-morrow we phlebotomize again;

Next day my new-invented patent draught:—
Then I have some pills prepared.
On Thursday we throw in the bark; on Friday—

Bal. [*Coming forward*, c.] Well, sir, on Friday—what on Friday? come,
Proceed—

Lam. Discovered!

Hostess. Mercy, noble sir!

[*They fall on their knees.*

Lam. We crave your mercy.

Bal. On your knees? 't is well!
Pray, for your time is short.

Hostess. Nay, do not kill us!

Bal. You have been tried, condemned, and only wait
For execution. Which shall I begin with?

Lam. The lady, by all means, sir!

Bal. Come, prepare. [*To the* HOSTESS.

Hostess. Have pity on the weakness of my sex!

Bal. Tell me, thou quaking mountain of gross flesh,
Tell me, and in a breath, how many poisons—
If you attempt it!—[*To* LAMPEDO, *who is endeavoring to make off*, L.]—you have cooked up for me?

Hostess. None, as I hope for mercy!

Bal. Is not thy wine a poison?

Hostess. No, indeed, sir!
'T is not, I own, of the first quality:
But—

Bal. What?

Hostess. I always give short measure, sir.
And ease my conscience that way.

Bal. Ease your conscience!
I 'll ease your conscience for you!

Hostess. Mercy, sir!

Bal. Rise, if thou can'st, and hear me.

Hostess. Your commands, sir?

Bal. If in five minutes all things are prepared
For my departure, you may yet survive.

Hostess. It shall be done in less.

Bal. Away, thou lump-fish! [*Exit* HOSTESS.

Lam. So, now comes my turn!—'t is all over with me!— [*Aside.*
There 's dagger, rope, and ratsbane in his looks.

Bal. And now, thou sketch and outline of a man!
Thou thing that hast no shadow in the sun!
Thou eel in a consumption, eldest born
Of Death and Famine! Thou anatomy
Of a starved pilchard!—

Lam. I do confess my leanness.—I am spare;
And therefore spare me!

Bal. Why, wouldst thou have made me
A thoroughfare for thy whole shop to pass through?

Lam. Man, you know, must live!

Bal. Yes: he must die, too.

Lam. For my patients' sake!

Bal. I 'll send you to the major part of them—
The window, sir, is open;—come, prepare—

Lam. Pray, consider!
I may hurt some one in the street.

Bal. Why, then, I'll rattle thee to pieces in a dice-box,
Or grind thee in a coffee-mill to powder;
For thou must sup with Pluto.—So, make ready,
Whilst I, with this good small-sword for a lancet,
Let thy starved spirit out—for blood thou hast none—
And nail thee to the wall, where thou shalt look
Like a dried beetle with a pin stuck through him.

Lam. Consider my poor wife!

Bal. Thy wife!

Lam. My wife, sir!

Bal. Hast thou dared think of matrimony, too?
No flesh upon thy bones, and take a wife!

Lam. I took a wife because I wanted flesh.
I have a wife and three angelic babes,
Who, by those looks, are well-nigh fatherless.

Bal. Well, well, your wife and children shall plead for you.
Come, come, the pills. Where are the pills? Produce them.

Lam. Here is the box.

Bal. Were it Pandora's, and each single pill
Had ten diseases in it, you should take them.

Lam. What, all?

Bal. Ay, all; and quickly, too!—Come, sir, begin.
[LAMPEDO *takes one*] That's well;—another.

Lam. One's a dose!

Bal. Proceed, sir!

Lam. What will become of me?—
Let me go home, and set my shop to rights,

And, like immortal Cæsar, die with decency.

Bal. Away! And thank thy lucky star I have not
Brayed thee in thy own mortar, or exposed thee
For a large specimen of the lizard genus.

Lam. Would I were one—for they can feed on air.

Bal. Home, sir! And be more honest.

Lam. If I am not,
I'll be more wise at least.

[*Exeunt* L., LAMPEDO 1*st*, BALTHAZAR, *threatening him*, 2*d*.

COSTUMES.

BALTHAZAR.—Drab jacket and trunks, trimmed with green ribbon bows and tin tags; grey wig.

LAMPEDO.—Black close-fitting suit; red stockings; black shoes; small three-cornered hat, and cane.

VOLANTE.—Handsome satin dress, with ornaments and feathers.

HOSTESS.—Black dress, with red points; point-lace apron, and cap.

THE HARVEST STORM.

A Domestic Drama.

FOR MALE CHARACTERS ONLY.

By C. H. Hazlewood.

PERSONS REPRESENTED.

JOHN GARNER, *an honest English farmer.*

DICK DARRELL, *a dissipated and unscrupulous yeoman.*

MR. LYNX, *a detective, and an honor to his profession.*

BARKER and NIBLER, *his assistants, sharp and decisive in action.*

SAMUEL LEXICON, *writing a new dictionary of the English language.*

ANDREW RADFORD, *clerk to a London banking-house, absconding—not from guilt, but from suspicion.*

MICHAEL, *brother to Andrew, and in the service of John Garner.*

CHARLEY COOPER, } *two Gipsies, with slight perceptions of the*
NAT LOVEL, } *difference between* "meum" *and* "tuum."

SCENE:—*Country View, with distant corn fields, Farm House* L., *Barn* R. 2 E. *Enter* MICHAEL *from farm. Music.*

Michael. Another fine day for the harvest; lucky weather, this, for the farmers, and I'm sure no one merits it more than my good master. I owe every thing to him; for when my parents died he became a second father to my brother and me; to me he gave shelter and education, and procured for my dear brother a clerk's situation at a banker's in London, where he has been these seven years. Good worthy master, may Providence smile upon your crops, and fill your barns with harvest's bounteous store. [*Takes letter from his pocket*] I have just received this letter from my brother, in which he tells me that his salary has again been raised; how happy it makes me to know that. He writes to me every week. I wonder when he 's coming to see us; I wish he was here now.

[*The barn door opens*, R. 2 E., *and* ANDREW RADFORD, *looking pale and agitated, enters from it.*

Andrew. He *is* here, Michael.

Michael. My dear Andrew! [*Taking his hand.*

Andrew. Hush, hush! not so loud, do n't mention my name, some one might hear you.

Michael. Not mention your name! why not?

Andrew. Brother, I am flying from justice, hide me, save me.

Michael. Flying from justice! Oh, what have you done? Is Andrew Radford, my brother, a hunted thief!

Andrew. No, Michael, no, I am as innocent as you are.

Michael. Then why dread your name being mentioned.

Andrew. Brother, listen to my story, then pity, believe, and assist me. At our bank in London, the clerks take it in turn to sleep in the room which contains the iron safe, wherein all the money, deeds, and securities are placed; last Thursday week it was my turn to sleep there, but scarcely had I entered the room when a sudden dizziness overtook me, and I remembered no more; the next morning I was roused by master and his partner, with the fearful news that the iron safe had been opened and its contents stolen. I was questioned; but bewildered and horrified, I knew not what I said. I was accused as the robber, my lodging searched, and there, secreted in my writing-desk, was found a bundle of notes that had been stolen from my master's house.

Michael. But you were innocent?

Andrew. As you are, Michael; but no one would believe me so; all looked on me with doubt and suspicion. I was given until the next day to confess my guilt or else be arrested on the charge of robbery. I knew I had no one to speak for me, I felt I was incapable of proving my innocence; so, in the dead of night, I fled.

Michael. Oh, rash and weak resolve! by doing that you have confirmed their suspicions.

Andrew. I feel I have, I see my folly. But it is now too late. I must gain some sea-port and sail for America—have you the means to help me to do so, brother?

Michael. Alas, no! all that I have is in our savings-bank, and can not be drawn out without notice. Meet this charge.

Andrew. I should be condemned as guilty, I am sure of it, all looks so black against me; time, I am assured, will prove my innocence, and then I can stand erect again in the eyes of the world; but if once I get the taint of a prison on me, I feel I should break down under it, and hear the world say the weight of my guilt had crushed me. Aid me, aid me, dear brother, to escape for the sake of *my* good name and your own!

Michael. I would willingly, if I had the means; but I have not. What can I do?

John. [*Within*] Michael, Michael, it's breakfast time, lad.

Michael. My master comes! Quick, Andrew, do not let him see you! [ANDREW *returns into barn.*

John. [*Entering from farm*] I've been looking for thee every where, my lad.

Michael. I heard you call, sir; I was just coming.

John. You seem scared—what's the matter?

Michael. I am not very well sir, I—I—Dear master, will you do me a favor? I never asked you one before.

John. Do thee a favor, Michael? Aye, that I will. What is it?

Michael. I want you to lend me ten pounds, master; you can stop it out of my wages.

John. What on earth can you want with ten pounds?

Michael. I want to lend it to a friend, sir.

John. Why you silly fellow! Dost think thou'd

ever see it again? What 's the name of the person who wants to borrow it of thee?

Michael. I should n't like to tell you that, sir; but it will do a young man I know a great deal of service; it will, indeed, master.

John. Well, let me know who the young man is, and what he wants the money for, and then perhaps, out of respect to you, I may let him have it.

Michael. You must excuse me telling you his name, sir.

John. Then you must excuse me lending you the money. No, no, my lad, I 'll not see you imposed upon; this is some new acquaintance of yours, who wants to wheedle you out of your little savings. Come in to breakfast; and do n't say another word on the subject, or else you 'll offend me. So come in with me, for I want thee. [*Exit into farm*, L.

Michael. [*Following him*] My poor brother! what will become of him?

[*Exit into farm*, L. *Enter* DICK DARRELL, *a young farmer*, R. U. E., *looking at farm.*

Dick. That farmer Garner 's a lucky man—never saw better crops in my life; he 's pretty warm, I warrant. Every thing he touches seems to prosper; while, on the contrary, all I meddle with goes wrong. To be sure, he does n't bet on horse-racing—I do; I suppose that makes all the difference. That Michael, who lives with him, I 'll warrant he 'll come into the best part of the old man's property—if I could only get round him he might help me to some of the farmer's money; but he does n't seem to cotton to me somehow.

[*Enter* SAMUEL LEXICON, *with note-book*, R. U. E.

Samuel. "Cotton." [*Writing in book*] "Cotton, a material from which shirts are made; and by which women easily make their fortune."

Dick. Were you listening to me, sir?

Samuel. Certainly not, sir; but, the fact is, I am compiling a new dictionary, forming a new signification to the English language, and I take the words as I hear them spoken—saves me a deal of trouble.

Dick. Oh, indeed! now I took you for some rascal of a lawyer.

Samuel. You do n't like lawyers, then?

Dick. No, I do n't; what 's your opinion of them?

Samuel. I 'll read it to you out of my dictionary. [*Reads*] "Lawyer, a learned gentleman, who rescues your estate from your enemies and keeps it himself."

Dick. True enough, my friend, for I know an instance of that; and to think of my taking you for a limb of the law! Excuse my oversight.

Samuel. Oversight! I have n't got that word. [*Writes in book*] "Oversight, leaving your old umbrella in a coffee-room and bringing away a new one in mistake."

Dick. [*Aside*] A curious fellow this. [*Aloud*] A stranger about here, I suppose?

Samuel. Yes, sir, merely traveling to pick up information.

Dick. Nice land about here.

Samuel. Beautiful! I suppose you've a tidy slice of it.

Dick. I had at one time, but I lost a good deal by speculation.

Samuel. [*Writes in book*] "Speculation, making your fortune by swindling your creditors, and then turning insolvent."

Dick. You see I spent a good deal on my land trying to improve it by science.

Samuel. [*Writing in book*] "Science, tying a tin canister to a dog's tail and observing which way he runs."

Dick. [*Aside*] I wonder who this is; he must be rich, or he would n't be so eccentric. [*Aloud*] Yes, sir, joke as you will, but science to a beginner in the farming line is a young man's best companion.

Samuel. Allow me to differ with you, this is my definition: [*Reads from book*] "Young man's best companion, a friend who sees you safe home when you 're unable to take yourself there."

Dick. [*Aside*] I see Michael coming, I wish I could get rid of him. [*Aloud*] If you wish to see the beauty of the country, sir, there 's a fine view when you get through the corn-fields.

Samuel. [*Looking*] Ah! I see, whose large red brick house is that yonder?

Dick. It belongs to Mr. Bowen, our magistrate.

Samuel. [*Writes in book*] "Magistrate, a worthy old gentleman, who goes to sleep all the time a case is being tried, then wakes up and says 'I see it all. Three months.'"

Dick. [*Aside*] Confound the fool, why do n't he go. [*Aloud*] I beg pardon, friend, but you are acting in a manner that—

Samuel. Acting! I beg your pardon, I 'm doing nothing of the kind. He takes me for an actor, a tragedian, perhaps! [*Writes in book*] "Tragedian, a fellow who runs about the stage with a tin pot on his head and gets into a passion, at so much a night." Well, I 'll be off, for I see you want to be left alone with your lady love. It 's the dairy-maid, I dare say. [*Writes in book*] "Dairy-maid, supposed by cockneys to be a rustic Venus; but who eats a pound of fat bacon for breakfast, and drinks a quart of table ale to wash it down." [*Going* R. U. E.] "Oh, that we can call these delicate creatures ours, and not their appetites."—Shakespeare! [*Exit*, R. U. E.

Dick. Gone at last, and here comes Michael.

[*Enter* MICHAEL *from farm.*

Michael. What can I do, how obtain the money? I dread every moment that my master will enter the barn and discover him. [*Aside.*

Dick. Good morning, Michael.

Michael. [*Starting*] Good morning, sir.

Dick. Sir! Why do n't you call me Dick, you 've known me long enough?

Michael. [*Aside*] I have, but never knew any thing to your credit, though.

Dick. I was wishing to speak to you, Michael.

I have been thinking that we ought to be good friends, and it shall not be my fault if we are not.

Michael. If you mean to abandon your bad and dissipated habits, so that one who respects himself can be your friend, I will be so; but until your actions give proof of this, I must beg you to let us continue as we are—not enemies, but certainly not friends.

Dick. "Certainly not friends."—How fine we talk, you ought to be proud of my notice, you who came here a friendless child.

Michael. Some people rise by industry, others fall by dissipation.

Dick. You 've a high spirit, my lad, but I may break it yet; since you will turn my good-will into hate, beware of me! [*Exit*, R. 1 E.

Michael. [*Watching him off*] He is gone. [*Goes to barn*] Andrew, you may venture, there is no one here.

Andrew. The money, quick; the torments of suspense—the fear of detection, make me tremble like a child.

Michael. Oh, my poor brother! what will you do? My master refuses to lend me the money, and I have no other friend I can ask.

Andrew. Then I am lost! I can not remain longer in concealment, and to venture on the road would be equally dangerous, for I feel assured the officers are on my track.

Michael. What can I do? Tell my master all?

No, I dread to do that, for so strict are his notions of justice that he would instantly order his arrest.

Andrew. [*Starts*] Hark! I hear footsteps.

Michael. Quick, conceal yourself!

[*Exit* ANDREW *to barn. Re-enter* DICK, R. 1 E., *with posting bill in his hand.*

Dick. You are still here, then? I am glad of it; I hold something in my hand that will crush your proud heart and level your pride to the earth, if I choose to make it known.

Michael. [*Aside*] What can he mean?

Dick. [*Shows bill*] I'll read you what is printed here—listen. [*Reads bill*] "£100 reward for the apprehension of Andrew Radford, late clerk in the employ of Sterling & Co., London, who is charged with robbery to a large amount. The above reward will be paid to any person or persons giving such information as may lead to his apprehension." [*To* MICHAEL, *who is agitated and trembling*] Ah! does my news strike home? You did n't think your brother was an outcast flying from justice, a wretched thief with a price set on his head!

Michael. Neither do I think so now, for I know he is innocent; this cloud which now hangs over my brother's name is but for a time, and I will trust to Heaven to clear his name, and reveal the guilty.

Dick. [*Going up*] So be it; since you are so boastful, I know what to do, and so I leave the thief's brother to his meditations. [*Exit,* L. U. E.

Michael. He will be captured; I shall be turned

from the farm, and my brother branded with crime! Oh, merciful Providence! what will be the end of this? [*Enter* MR. LYNX, *a detective*, R. U. E.

Mr. L. [*Looking about*] Burton Farm, near the five-acre field, this must be the place. Good morning, does one Mr. John Garner, a farmer, live hereabouts?

Michael. Yes, sir, in yonder farm.

Mr. L. Do you know one Michael Radford, who lives with him as servant?

Michael. I am Michael Radford, sir.

Mr. L. Indeed! now answer me truly, for I assure you it will be to your advantage to tell me all you know. Have you seen your brother lately? I want him, I 'm a detective from London.

Michael. [*Starting, aside*] A detective! [*Aloud*] My brother? I regret that it is not in my power to afford you any information regarding him.

Mr. L. You are certain? Be sure of what you say, for much depends on the truth of your answer.

Michael. I have already told you, sir, that I can not direct you to his retreat.

Mr. L. Well, I 'll take your word, but if you are deceiving me you 'll be sorry for it, I assure you, my dear fellow.

[*Enter* SAMUEL LEXICON, *overhearing the last words*, R. U. E.

Samuel. [*Writing in book*] "Dear fellow"—dear, an expression used by man and wife at the commencement of a quarrel."

Mr. L. [*To* MICHAEL] If you should see your master about, say I wish to speak to him, will you?

Michael. I will, sir. [*Going up to house and looking toward barn unobserved*] He is lost!

[*Exit in farm,* L.

Mr. L. [*To* SAMUEL] Nice weather, sir.

Samuel. [*Writing in book*] "Weather, an uncertain article, sure to be very wet if you go out with a new hat on, and very bright and fine if you go out in your old one and carry an umbrella."

Mr. L. An artist, I presume.

Samuel. You do presume, sir, and I am not an artist; no, sir, I am a lexicographer.

Mr. L. Oh, I see, one of those chaps who take likenesses, and hang a board outside their shops, "A portrait and a black-pudding for a penny."

Samuel. [*Writing in book*] "Black-pudding, a mysterious article of food, supposed to be composed of bullock's blood and sawdust." But allow me to correct you, sir, I said a lexicographer not a photographer—one illustrates words, the other faces. May I be allowed to ask what you are?

Mr. L. I am a detective.

Samuel. [*Writes in book*] "Detective, one who puts down thieves by taking them up."

Mr. L. But to business. Have you seen a suspicious looking character about here?

Samuel. Nobody but yourself.

Mr. L. Oh, you flatter me.

Samuel. No, I don't, I'm speaking the truth, I

am indeed; do n't be offended, you ought to feel proud at an author taking notice of you—author! I have n't got that word. [*Writes in book*] "Author, a man who writes a lot of lies every week, and kills people in penny numbers."

[*Enter* JOHN GARNER, *from farm*, L.

John. [*To* MR. LYNX] I hear you wish to speak with me, sir.

Mr. L. Yes; your servant Michael has a brother named Andrew Radford, I believe.

John. Quite right, and an honest young man he is. I recommended him to his present employers in London.

Mr. L. I am aware of it, have you seen him lately?

John. Not these three months.

Mr. L. Are you certain?

John. Positive! Why do you doubt my word? I never lie to any man; what is your business?

Mr. L. That must be told in secret.

John. Will you step into the house?

Mr. L. No, I have no time to stay.

John. Well, I am going round the farm, will you walk with me?

Mr. L. I will.

John. This way then. [*Going up*, R. U. E.] We can talk as we go.

Mr. L Not here; silence until we are alone.

[*Exeunt*, R. U. E.

Samuel. [*Writes in book*] "Silence, a thing never

to be found where three women are." If this book do n't astonish the literary world, I am much mistaken. My dictionary goes straight to the point and tells people the real meaning of the words. I wonder how many I 've got down.

[*Looks over his book. Enter* CHARLEY COOPER *and* NAT LOVEL, *two Gipsies, observing him, from* L. U. E.

Nat. [*Aside to* CHARLEY] I thought you told me there was nobody here; who 's that chap?

Charley. You do n't call him any body do you? Let 's chaff him. [*They advance on each side.*

Nat. [*Slaps* SAMUEL *on shoulder*] Hope you 're well, sir.

Charley. [*Slaps* SAMUEL *on the other*] The aforesaid, sir.

Samuel. [*Looks at them*] Gipsies! I have n't got them in my dictionary. [*Writes in book*] "Gipsies, mahogany coffee-colored people; supposed to be able to read the stars and tell fortunes, but in reality the greatest liars and thieves under the sun."

Nat and *Charley.* Hollo, hollo, mate, draw it mild!

Samuel. No, I shall not draw it mild; mine 's a dictionary that shall tell people what they really are in plain English.

Nat. How dare you take away our characters?

Samuel. Really, gentlemen, I was not aware you had any!

Nat. [*Draws knife*] Do you know what this is?

Charley. [*Drawing another*] And do you know what this is, and what it 's likely to do?

Samuel. Yes; what I 'm going to do.

Charley. And what 's that?

Samuel. Cut! [*Runs off*, R. U. E.

Nat. [*Looks after him*] Ha, ha, ha! yonder he goes. I thought he would n't chop logic with us long; if he had, I 'd have chopped his ears off. [*Looks round*] Nobody seems about. Now 's our time!

Charley. To business then! You say the old farmer always has money in the house?

Nat. Heaps! Our Nell came round yesterday to observe the premises, under the pretense of selling cabbage-nets and telling fortunes. She tells me she peeped in at the window, and twigged the old man counting his money into the cash box; and it was all in gold, my lad; think of that! no numbered notes to nail a chap; but shining gold!—lovely canaries that we must fly off with!

Charley. Is there ever a dog on the premises likely to spoil us?

Nat. Not one, and all the people are in the fields as busy as bees.

Charley. How grateful we ought to be to Providence for being so kind to us. Follow me, and let us sneak in. [*They go toward house and peep in*] Hold hard! here 's somebody. To cover! to cover!

[*They conceal themselves behind house.*

Michael. [*Entering from farm, with food in basket*]

I wonder if I can take this to my brother unperceived? How I long to save him from the crime which is so unjustly laid to his charge. But what chance, what hope have I of doing so? But yet I must!—I will save him at all hazards! for his capture and disgrace would be my death. But courage, Michael, courage! he is not taken yet; and if I can but secure his safety until to-morrow, I'll go into the town and try every friend I have in the world, but I'll raise the money he requires for his escape! There seems to be no one about; now, then, is the time to venture.

[*Music. Goes cautiously into barn. Re-enter* NAT *and* CHARLEY.

Nat. Now's our time, quick does it.

[*They exeunt into farm. Enter* MR. LYNX *and* JOHN GARNER, R. U. E.

John. Can it be possible!

Mr. L. I thought my news would surprise you, farmer.

John. Whoever would have thought it? I hope you are convinced that I can not tell you where to find Andrew.

Mr. L. Perfectly, or else you would, I am assured.

John. Why not see his brother and ask him?

Mr. L. I have already done so, and he, like you, says he does not know where he is to be found.

John. It's the strangest affair I've heard of for some time.

Mr. L. I thought it would astonish you; for my

own part it 's as queer a case as ever I was employed upon.

John. Well, but do you think there is no way to find him?—look here.

[*They talk together in dumb show. Enter* NAT *and* CHARLEY, *from farm, with bags of money and cash box; they steal off*, R. U. E.

John. Do you mean to continue your search?

Mr. L. I never give up my game till I 've run it down.

John. I trust you may find him, and that speedily.

Mr. L. Trust me for that; I 'm Lynx by name and lynx by nature. Let 's in and question the lad again.

John. If he knows any thing, depend on his telling you.

Mr. L. Not till he 's heard my news, I'm afraid; but I 'll try him.

[*They exeunt in farm. Re-enter* DICK DARRELL, R. U. E.

Dick. If I have n't had my way with Michael, at least I 've had my revenge; there 's two officers down at the Barley Mow from London, and they swear they 'll have him if he 's in the country. Now, Michael Radford, your proud spirit will soon rue the day when you insulted Dick Darrell.

[*Re-enter* JOHN *and* MR. LYNX, *from farm. Music.*

John. Ruin, beggary, poverty! stares me in the face; for I have been robbed—robbed of all I had in the world.

Mr. L. The cleanest thing I ever heard of, when did you last see the money safe?

John. When I rose this morning. Let search be made every-where; you are an officer, tell me what is to be done, for Heaven's sake?

Dick. What 's the matter?

John. I am robbed, Richard—robbed of every penny I had in the world; it was but yesterday I drew it from the bank to place it in the London one, and I find it gone! gone!

Dick. But where was Michael, your careful favorite?

John. Aye, true, true; why did he leave the farm?

Dick. Why, indeed! if he do n't know something of it I 'm a Dutchman.

[SAMUEL *re-entering*, R. U. E.

Samuel. Bless me, what 's the matter? your faces seem as full of meaning as my dictionary.

Mr. L. There 's been a thief on the premises.

Samuel. [*Writes in book*] "Thief, a dishonest character; a rogue, who is better fed and treated than many poor paupers are."

[MICHAEL *is seen to enter from barn, and tries to enter the farm unperceived.*

John. [*Turning and seeing him*] Michael! how is this? why are you out of the house? you have been my ruin; for by your carelessness, my house has been robbed of every penny.

Michael. Robbed! no, no, master; impossible! it was but this moment that I left all safe.

John. What business could have taken you into the barn?

Dick. Aye, what indeed?

Mr. L. This looks very strange, young man.

Michael. Why do you all look at me in this manner? Surely you do not think that I know any thing of this?

Mr. L. What is your master to think, when knowing that there is a large sum of money in the house, you leave the premises without a soul to take care of them?

Michael. Master! master, do n't think, pray do n't, that I know a word of this villainy; you do n't think so? I 'm sure you do n't. Oh! let me at least hear you say that.

John. What can I think, Michael? no one but you knew where my money was kept.

Michael. But why should I rob you? what need have I of money?

John. What need had you of the ten pounds, you wanted to borrow of me a short time ago?

Michael. [*Confused*] Oh! that—I—I wanted for —for—

John. For what?

Michael. Oh! I can not, dare not tell you.

Dick. [*To* LYNX] You see how the case is?

Mr. L. I 'm afraid I do, I 've seen too many cases of the same kind not to understand all this. A good and virtuous youth, as I hear he has been, forms an acquaintance with some crafty fellow; let's him have the run of the house when his master 's out, and in return he runs off with the cash box—a common case. My experience tells me that a thief seldom carries so large a sum with him, but hides it; so my plan is to search the premises; let 's look over the barn in the first place.

[*Going to barn*, MICHAEL *places himself before it.*

Michael. No—no, there is nothing there, indeed there is not.

Mr. L. Well, if there is nothing there, why should you mind my searching for it?

Dick. [*To* JOHN] What do you think of Master Innocence now?

Samuel. [*Writes in book*] "Innocence, a thing we all possess till we 're found out."

John. Michael, if you do not wish me to think you guilty, stand from the door.

Michael. I can not—I will not, your money is not there; but still you must not enter.

Mr. L. [*Aside*] I see we shall have a tough job with this fellow. [*To* SAMUEL] Oblige me by stepping down to the Barley Mow, and asking my brother constables to come here, and bring their handcuffs with them.

Samuel. [*Writing in book*] "Handcuffs, heavy steel bracelets for light fingers." I'm off like the first edition of my dictionary. [*Exit*, R. U. E.

John. Stand aside, Michael.

Michael. No—no, master, [*kneels*] in mercy take my word, that not one penny is in the barn; yet I do not wish you to enter—why, I dare not tell you; but here, under the broad sky, in the face of Heaven and man, I swear that I am guiltless of robbing my kind old master.

Dick. Oh, this is child's play; if you won't force him from the door, I will. Out of my way, or I'll make you. Stand aside, thief!

[*As he advances to seize him,* ANDREW *hastily enters from barn and knocks him down.*

John. Andrew! And here!

Andrew. Could I bear more? could I listen longer to the taunts and accusing words that proclaimed my brother and myself dishonest? No, I am here; do with me what you please, for the two brothers will brave their fate together.

[*Re-enter* SAMUEL, R. U. E.

Samuel. Your brother's innocent if you're not; for your brother officers [*to* LYNX] have caught the real thieves with the money in their possession, and here they come with it.

[*Enter* BARKER *and* NIBLER, *bringing on* COOPER *and* LOVEL, *handcuffed,* R. U. E.

Barker. [*Gives money to* JOHN] This money is yours, I believe; be kind enough to attend before the magistrate in the morning to give evidence against the men if you please.

Charley. Well I'm blessed! you're not agoing to persecute us in that way for next to nothing. We did n't mean to prig it, not by no means; we only took it to see how fur we could carry it without dropping it. It was a wager betwixt us. I bet Nat here, a tanner, that I could carry it furder than he could bring it back, and you grabbed us both afore I had carried it half as far as I could.—It was only a wager.—You would n't go for to lag a poor cove for a wager, would you now?

Mr. L. Away with them, we know something else of you. You 'll get a traveling ticket, you may be sure of it. Off with them.

Charley. Well then, blow you all, that 's what I say. I shall hemigrate, I won't give a cuss to stay in a country vot persecutes the hindustrious poor in this way. Come, Nat, keep up your courage; we shall only have fourteen years' board and lodging for nothing. So off we goes, and blow the expense.

[*They are taken off*, R. U. E.

Michael. Oh! joyful event, that clears my good name in the eyes of all.

Dick. But still your brother 's guilty.

Mr. L. How do you know he 's guilty?

Dick. Why is n't there a reward offered for him?

Mr. L. There was yesterday, but there is not to-day.

Michael and *Andrew.* No?

Dick. Why how is that?

Mr. L. [*To* DICK] The real robber confessed his guilt this morning at the Mansion House, he was a fellow clerk of this young man's; and on the night he had to guard the bank, he drugged the drink, plundered the strong-room, and by the aid of an accomplice placed some of the notes at his lodgings —and that shuts up your note, I believe, my friend.

John. Andrew, my lad, thou art the honest fellow I always took thee for.

Andrew. My kind, my earliest friend.

Dick. Well! this is a strange go.

Samuel. [*Writes in book*] "Go, a word of one syllable, which some people would be wise to adopt, before they are kicked out."

Dick. Curse me, if I ever enter the village again.

[*Exit*, R. 1 E.

Samuel. For which the village ought to be very much obliged to you.

John. [*Taking a hand each of* MICHAEL *and* ANDREW] Andrew and Michael, you shall be my heirs; the money I will leave you must prosper threefold in your hands, for it has been gained honestly, and may every honest lad meet with a friend like me to help them.

Michael. I see friends around me on every side, whose bright looks tell me that we have reaped their praise and gained their smiles, and if a few clouds gathered over our Harvest Moon, Providence has dispersed the storm, we hope, forever.

Short is the date in which ill acts prevail.
But honesty's a rock can never fail.

Curtain.

VAN DUNDERMAN AND HIS SERVANT.

From the Blacksmith of Antwerp, by John O'Keefe.

PERSONS REPRESENTED.

HERR VAN DUNDERMAN. JACOB.

SCENE:—*A Room. Enter* DUNDERMAN, *elegantly dressed, but with a night-cap on. He has a pipe in his mouth.*

Dun. Vere is dis coach! [*Looks at his watch*] 'T is now past twelve, and I should be at Van Dipenbeck's house—I tink I look very well in my wedding suit!—How long dis coach stay, and my sweet bride is vait for me.—Vat a deal of pictures I have here unfinished, but no matter, I vil not paint to-day. [*Calls*] Here,—Yacob,—my man Yacob!—Ah, dis new servant!—I ave him only two days, and he put all of my affairs into confusion; he is always ready too soon, or he is not ready at all; he underdoes, or he overdoes. [*Calls*] Yacob!—No, he vil not do for me. [*Enter* JACOB] Hey, you Yacob, is dis coach not come?

Jacob. Not yet, sir, and I desired him to be here exactly at one.

Dun. One! and I desired you to bid him come at eleven—when I give you a message, mind always say my words exactly.

Jacob. Yes, sir, I will, sir; but here, sir, my lord is come; he says this is the day you appointed to take a sitting of him.

Dun. I will not draw any body's picture on my wedding-day; so he may take his ugly face somewhere else.

Jacob. [*Goes to the door and speaks loud*] My lord, you may take your ugly face somewhere else.

Dun. Vile loot! Vat you talk dat vay to my patrons?

Jacob. Why, sir, was n't that speaking your words exactly. There 's my Lady Frinsmere below stairs, too; she wants to sit.

Dun. Let her sit in the great chair below, and when she 's tired of sitting, let her waddle off.

Jacob. [*Calling at the entrance*] My lady, sit below, in the great chair, and when you 're tired, waddle off.

Dun. Vat you mean? Let my customers alone, since you can't talk good manners to dem—[*A knocking without.* JACOB *going*]—Stop, [*in a lower tone*] if that 's Captain Lillo, do n't say I 'm at home.

Jacob. [*Whispering*] I won't, I won't, sir.

[*Exit.*

Dun. He wants to be my bridesman, and I do not like captains for my bridesman.

[*Busies himself about the room. Re-enter* JACOB.

Jacob. [*In a low tone*] Sir, I told him what you bid me, and he 's in the next room writing a card to leave for you.

Dun. What, what? I hate whispering.

Jacob. [*Very loud*] Sir, Captain Lillo 's in the next room, and I told him you was n't at home, as you desired me.

Dun. Hush! de deuce is in your tongue! How I am perplexed and vexed at this time; but let me get out of de house.—Vy did you say I vas at home to all dese peoples?

Jacob. Why, lord, sir, one does n't know what to do with you! I do n't know when to tell lies, nor when to tell truth.

Dun. Mind, Yacob, tell lies to all de world, but truth to your master.

Jacob. I shall, sir.

Dun. Here fetch my wig, [*takes off night-cap and puts on wig*] do n't break my pipe—dere, dat vil do; Yacob, I make a tolerable smart bridegroom, eh! I tink I look very well to-day.

Jacob. Indeed, sir, day or night, you look frightful always.

Dun. Eh, vat is dat! vat you say such a rude ting to me for?

Jacob. You bid me always speak truth to my master.

Dun. Yes, but you should not be so ready vid your tongue.

Jacob. I won't, sir. I hear the coach stop.

Dun. De coach! Come, den, I must light a fresh pipe to take vid me; mind, have a guard over your speech; you should tink three times before you speak once.

[*Lights his pipe, and stands near the candle.*

Jacob. I shall, sir; I think once, I think twice, I think three times,—your wig 's on fire.

Dun. [*Strikes him*] Ah, you scoundrel! you rascal!

Jacob. Help, fire, murder.

[*Exeunt*, JACOB *running*, DUNDERMAN *pursuing.*

COSTUMES.

VAN DUNDERMAN.—Knee-breeches with wide legs; silk stockings; ornamented long vest, with full sleeves; elegant mantle; large, ruff-like, lace collar, with long points, forming a complete circle about the neck; dress-sword; fancy slippers; periwig.

JACOB.—Close-fitting breeches; red stockings; dark shoes; tight waistcoat, buttoned to the chin; very short hair.

THE HEARTLESS LANDLORD.

From Douglas Jerrold's Black-Eyed Susan.

PERSONS REPRESENTED.

DOGGRASS. BLACK-EYED SUSAN.
GNATBRAIN. DOLLY MAYFLOWER.
JACOB TWIG.

SCENE:—*A Cottage Interior. Practicable door and lattice window in left flat.* (D. L. F.) *Set door at second entrance on the right. Enter* SUSAN, R.

Susan. Twelve long and tedious months are passed, and no tidings of William. Shame upon the unkind hearts that parted us—that sent my dear husband to dare the perils of the ocean, and made me a pining, miserable creature! Oh, the pangs, the dreadful pangs that tear the sailor's wife, as, wakeful on her tear-wet pillow, she lists and trembles at the roaring sea! [*Enter* GNAT. *at the cottage door*, L. C.

Gnat. There she is, like a caged nightingale, singing her heart out at her prison-bars—for this cottage is little better than a jail to her. Susan!

Susan. Gnatbrain!

Gnat. In faith, Susan, if sorrow makes such sweet music, may I never turn skylark, but always remain a goose.

Susan. Have you seen my uncle?

Gnat. Oh, yes!

Susan. Will he show any kindness?

Gnat. I can not tell. You may have flowers from an aloe-tree, if you wait a hundred years.

Susan. He has threatened to distress the good dame.

Gnat. Ay, for the rent. Oh, Susan, I would I were your landlord! I should think myself well paid if you would allow me every quarter-day to put my ear to the key-hole, and listen to one of your prettiest ditties. Why, for such payment, were I your landlord, I 'd find you in board, washing, and lodging, and the use of a gig on Sundays. I wish I—but la! what 's the use of my wishing? I 'm nobody but half-gardener, half-waterman—a kind of alligator, that gets his breakfast from the shore, and his dinner from the sea—a— [*Voice without.*

Susan. Oh, begone! I see Mr. Doggrass; if he find you here—

Gnat. He must not; here's a cupboard—I'm afraid there's plenty of room in it.

Susan. No, no, I would not for the world—there is no occasion—meet him.

Gnat. Not I, for quiet's sake. We never meet but, like fire and gunpowder, there is an explosion. This will do.

[*Goes into the closet*, R. 2 E. *Enter* DOGGRASS, D. F. L.

Dog. Now, Susan, you know my business—I say, you know my business? I come for money.

Susan. I have none, sir.

Dog. A pretty answer, truly. Are people to let their houses to beggars?

Susan. Beggars! Sir, I am your brother's orphan child.

Dog. I am sorry for it. I wish he were alive to pay for you. And where is your husband?

Susan. Do *you* ask where he is? I am poor, sir—poor and unprotected—do not, as you have children of your own—do not insult me. [*Weeps.*

Dog. Ay, this it is to let houses to women; if the tax-gatherer could be paid with crying, why, nobody would roar more lustily than myself. Let a man ask for his rent, and you pull out your pocket-handkerchief. Where's Dame Hatley?

Susan. In the next room—ill, very ill.

Dog. An excuse to avoid me; she shall not.

[*Going*, R.

Susan. You will not enter?

Dog. Who shall stop me?

Susan. If Heaven give me power—I! Uncle, the old woman is sick—I fear dangerously. Her spirit, weakened by late misfortune, flickers, like a dying light—your sudden appearance might make all dark. Uncle—*landlord!* would you have murder on your soul?

Dog. Murder?

Susan. Yes; though such may not be the common word: hearts are daily crushed, spirits broken—whilst he who slays, destroys in safety.

Dog. Can Dame Hatley pay me the money?

Susan. No.

Dog. Then she shall to prison.

Susan. She will die there.

Dog. Well!

Susan. Would you make the old woman close her eyes in a jail?

Dog. I have no time to hear sentiment. Mrs. Hatley has no money—you have none. Well, though she does n't merit lenity of me, I 'll not be harsh with her. [*Enter* DOLLY MAYFLOWER, D. F. L.

Susan. I thought you could not.

Dog. I 'll take whatever may be in the house, and will put up with the rest of the loss.

Dolly. So, Mr. Doggrass, this is how you behave to unfortunate folks—coming and selling them up, and turning them out. Is this your feeling for the poor?

Dog. Feeling! I pay the rates. What business have you here? Go to your spinning.

Dolly. Spinning! if it were to spin a certain wicked old man a halter, I'd never work faster. Ugh! I always thought you very ugly, but now you look hideous.

Susan. Peace, good Dolly.

Dolly. Peace! Oh, you are too quiet—too gentle! Take example by me: I only wish he'd come to sell me up, that's all. [DOGGRASS *goes to door*] Oh, I know who you are looking for—your man, Jacob Twig; he hops after you on your dirty work, like a tomtit after a jackdaw. I saw him leering in at the door. I wish my dear Gnatbrain was here. Oh, Susan, I wish he was here! He's one of the best, most constant of lovers—he'd befriend you for my sake.

Dog. [*Goes to the door*] Jacob! [*Enter* JACOB TWIG, D. F. L.] You know your business.

Jacob. What, here, master?—what, at old Dame Hatley's?

Dolly. To be sure, good Jacob; if your master had a tree, and but one squirrel lived in it, he'd take its nuts, sooner than allow it lodging gratis.

Susan. Uncle, have compassion—wait but another week—a day.

Dog. Not an hour—a minute. Jacob, do your duty. Now begin, put down every thing you see in the cottage.

Jacob. Master, hadn't you better wait a little?

Perhaps the dame can find friends. [DOGGRASS *is imperative*] Well, here goes; I'll first begin with the cupboard.

Susan. [*Anxiously*] No, let me entreat you do not. Come this way, if you are determined.

Dog. Eh! why that way? why not with the cupboard? I suspect—

Jacob. And now, so do I.

Dolly. You suspect! I dare say. Suspicion is all your brain can manage. What should you suspect—a thing that never had a thought deeper than a mug of ale? You suspect Susan! Why, we shall have the crows suspecting the lilies.

Jacob. You say so, do you? Now, I'll show you my consequence. I'll put every thing down, master, and begin with the cupboard. Ah! it's fast; I'll have it open—and I'll put the first thing down.

[*Pulls open the door, when* GNATBRAIN *knocks* JACOB *down with rolling-pin, puts his foot upon him, and stands,* R. 2 E., *in attitude.* SUSAN *in* R. *corner.* DOLLY, L. C., *in surprise.* DOGGRASS *standing in corner, exulting.*

Gnat. No, I'll put the first thing down.

Dolly. Gnatbrain! Oh, Susan, Susan!

Dog. Oh, Oh! we shall have the crows suspecting the lilies! Pretty flower! how it hangs its head! Go on with your duty, Jacob; put down every thing in the house.

Gnat. Do, Jacob; and begin with "one broken head"—then, write one stony-hearted landlord—one young woman innocent—ditto, jealous, [*squinting at* DOLLY]—one man tolerably honest—and one somewhat damaged.

Jacob. I 'll have you up before justices—you have broken my crown.

Gnat. Broken your crown! Jacob, Jacob! it was cracked before.

Jacob. How do you know that?

Gnat. By the ring of it, Jacob, by the ring: I never heard such a bit of *Brummagem* in my life.

Dog. [*To* SUSAN] Well, Susan, it is sometimes convenient for a husband to be at sea?

Susan. Sir, scorn has no words, contempt no voice to speak my loathing of your insinuations. Take, sir, all that is here—satisfy your avarice; but dare not indulge your malice at the cost of one, who has now nothing left her in her misery but the sweet consciousness of virtue. [*Exit*, R. H.

Dog. The way with all women when they are found out, is it not, Mrs. Dolly?

Dolly. I can't tell, sir; I never was found out.

Dog. Ay, you are lucky.

Dolly. Yes—we do n't meet often. But as for you, Mr. Gnatbrain—

Gnat. Now, no insinuations. I wish I could remember what Susan said about virtue: it would apply to my case admirably. Nothing like a sentiment to stop a charge—one may apply it to a bleeding reputation, as barbers do cobwebs to a wound.

Dog. Jacob, do you stay here—see that nothing of the least value leaves the house.

Gnat. In that case, Jacob, you may let your master go out.

Dog. Some day, my friend, I shall be a match for you.

[DOGGRASS *shakes stick at* GNATBRAIN, *and exit* D. F. L. GNATBRAIN *throws the rolling-pin at him, and then pursues* JACOB *into* R. *corner.*

Gnat. Perhaps so, but one of us must change greatly to make us pairs. Jacob, I never look upon your little carcass, but it reminds me of a pocket edition of the Newgate Calendar—a neat Old Bailey duodecimo. You are a most villainous looking rascal—an epitome of a noted highwayman.

Jacob. What?

Gnat. True as the light. You have a most Tyburn-like physiognomy—there 's Turpin in the curl of your upper lip—Jack Sheppard in the under one—your nose is Jerry Abershaw himself—Duval and Barrington are in your eyes—and, as for your chin, why Sixteen-String Jack lives again in it. [GNATBRAIN *goes to window,* L. F., *affecting to see what is passing outside*] Eh! well done—excellent! there 's all the neighbors getting the furniture out the garden window.

Jacob. Is there? It 's against the law. I 'm his Majesty's officer, and I 'll be among them in a whistle.

[*Exit* D. F. L. GNATBRAIN *instantly bolts it.*

Gnat. A bailiff, like a snow-storm, is always best on the outside. Now, Dolly, sweet Dolly Mayflower.

Dolly. Do n't talk to me, sir! The cupboard, sir, the cupboard.

Gnat. Hear my defense. I had not the least idea that you would have looked there, or the cupboard is the very last place I should have gone into.

Dolly. It 's no matter; there 's Mr. James Rattlin, boatswain's mate of the Bellerophon—

Gnat. What! you would n't marry a sailor?

Dolly. And why not?

Gnat. Your natural timidity would n't allow you.

Dolly. My timidity?

Gnat. Your husband would be at sea six months out of the twelve; there would be a wintry prospect for you.

Dolly. But he would be at home the other six—and there 's summer, sir.

Gnat. True, but when you can have summer all the year round, do n't you think it more to your advantage?

Dolly. No—for, if it always shone, we should never really enjoy fine weather.

Gnat. Oh, my dear, when we are married, we 'll get up a thunder-storm or two, depend upon it. But come, Dolly, your heart is too good, your head too clear, to nourish idle suspicions. Let us go and see poor Susan. There is real calamity enough in our every-day paths; we need not add to it by our own caprice. [*Exeunt*, L.

COSTUMES.

GNATBRAIN.—Blue jacket; nankeen trousers; white hat; and gardener's blue apron.

JACOB TWIGG.—Green trousers; short green coat; and white waistcoat; with white beaver hat.

DOGGRASS.—Brown coat, breeches, and waistcoat; with three-cornered hat.

SUSAN.—A brown open gown; white petticoat; and muslin apron; with white gypsy hat, trimmed with pink.

DOLLY MAYFLOWER.—A country girl's dress.

THE PEDANT.

From The Mistake, by Vanburgh.

PERSONS REPRESENTED.

Don Alvarez, *an irascible old gentleman.*
Metaphrastus, *tutor to Alvarez's son.*

Scene:—*An Apartment. Enter* Don Alvarez.

Alv. I'll try if I can discover, by his tutor, what it is that seems so much to work his brain of late; for something more than common there plainly does appear, yet nothing sure that can disturb his soul like what I have to torture mine upon his account. Sure nothing in this world is worth a troubled mind. What racks has avarice stretched me on! I wanted nothing: kind Heaven had given me a plenteous lot, and seated me in great abundance. I have bartered peaceful days for restless nights; a wretched bargain! and he that merchandizes thus must be undone at last. [*Enter* Metaphrastus.

Met. *Mandatum tuum curo diligenter.*

Alv. Master, I had a mind to ask you—

Met. The title master, comes from *Magis* and *Ter*, which is as much as to say, thrice worthy.

Alv. I never heard so much before, but it may be true, for aught I know. But, master—

Met. Go on.

Alv. Why, so I will, if you'll let me, but do n't interrupt me, then.

Met. Enough, proceed.

Alv. Why, then, master, for a third time, my son Camillo gives me much uneasiness of late; you know I love him, and have many careful thoughts about him.

Met. 'T is true. *Filio non potest præferri nisi filius.*

Alv. Master, when one has business to talk on, these scholastic expressions are not of use; I believe you a great Latinist; possibly you may understand Greek: those who recommend you to me said so, and I am willing it should be true; but the thing I want to discourse you about at present, does not properly give you an occasion to display your learning. Besides, to tell you truth, 't will at all times be lost upon me; my father was a wise man, but he taught me nothing beyond common sense; I know but one tongue in the world, which luckily being understood by you as well as me, I fancy, whatever thoughts we have to communicate to one another, may reasonably be conveyed in that, without having recourse to the language of Julius Cæsar.

Met. You are wrong, but may proceed.

Alv. I thank you: what is the matter I do not know; but, though it is of the utmost consequence to me to marry my son, what match soever I propose to him, he still finds some pretense or other to decline it.

Met. He is, perhaps, of the humor of a brother of Marcus Tullius, who—

Alv. Dear master, leave the Greeks, and the Latins, and the Scotch, and the Welsh, and let me go on in my business; what have those people to do with my son's marriage?

Met. Again you are wrong; but go on.

Alv. I say, then, that I have strong apprehensions, from his refusing all my proposals, that he may have some secret inclination of his own: and, to confirm me in this fear, I yesterday observed him (without his knowing it) in a corner of the grove, where nobody comes—

Met. A place out of the way, you would say; a place of retreat.

Alv. Why, the corner of the grove, where nobody comes, is a place of retreat, is it not?

Met. In Latin, *Secessus.*

Alv. Ha!

Met. As Virgil has it, *Est in secessu locus.*

Alv. How could Virgil have it, when I tell you no soul was there but he and I?

Met. Virgil is a famous author; I quote his saying as a phrase more proper to the occasion than that you use, and not as one who was in the wood with you.

Alv. And I tell you, I hope to be as famous as

any Virgil of 'em all, when I have been dead as long, and have no need of a better phrase than my own to tell you my meaning.

Met. You ought, however, to make choice of the words most used by the best authors. *Tu vivendo bonos*, as they say, *Scribendo sequare peritos.*

Alv. Again!

Met. 'T is Quintilian's own precept.

Alv. Zounds!—

Met. And he hath something very learned upon it, that may be of service to you to hear.

Alv. You ill-mannered rascal, will you hear me speak?

Met. What may be the occasion of this unmanly passion? What is it you would have with me?

Alv. What you might have known an hour ago, if you had pleased.

Met. You would, then, have me hold my peace? —I shall.

Alv. You will do very well.

Met. You see I do; well, go on.

Alv. Why, then, to begin once again, I say my son Camillo—

Met. Proceed; I sha' n't interrupt you.

Alv. I say my son Camillo—

Met. What is it you say of your son Camillo?

Alv. That he has got a dog of a tutor, whose brains I 'll beat out, if he won't hear me speak.

Met. That dog is a philosopher, contemns passion, and yet will hear you.

Alv. I do n't believe a word on 't, but I 'll try once again; I have a mind to know from you, whether you have observed any thing in my son—

Met. Nothing that is like his father. Go on.

Alv. Have a care.

Met. I do not interrupt you; but you are long in coming to a conclusion.

Alv. Why, thou hast not let me begin yet.

[*Crosses over.*

Met. And yet 't is high time to have made an end.

Alv. Dost thou know thy danger? I have not—thus much patience left.

[*Showing the end of his finger.*

Met. Mine is already consumed. I do not use to be thus treated; my profession is to teach, and not to hear, yet I have harkened like a school-boy, and am not heard, although a master.

Alv. Get out of the room.

Met. I will not. If the mouth of a wise man be shut, he is, as it were, a fool; for who shall know his understanding? therefore a certain philosopher said well, Speak, that thou mayest be known; great talkers, without knowledge, are as the winds that whistle; but they who have learning, should speak aloud. If this be not permitted, [ALVAREZ *manifests increasing impatience, walking to and fro, and at length seizes a large bell from the table*] we may expect to see the whole order of nature overthrown; hens devour foxes, and lambs destroy wolves; generals mend stockings, and chamber-maids take towns: we may expect, I say—

Alv. That, and that, and that, and—

[*Strikes him, and kicks him, and then follows him off violently ringing the bell at his ear.*

Met. *O, Tempora! O, Mores!*

COSTUMES.

DON ALVAREZ.—Gray tunic reaching to the knees, with one or two puffs or broad ruffles at the top of the sleeves; short cloak with square cape; buff tights; slippers with rosettes; thin gray hair, mustache, and whiskers.

METAPHRASTUS.—Long dressing-gown; bald head; spectacles.

CARATACH AND HENGO.

From Beaumont and Fletcher's Bonduca.

PERSONS REPRESENTED.

CARATACH, *general of the Britons.*
HENGO, *a brave boy, nephew to Caratach.*
MACER, *a Roman officer.*
JUDAS, *a cowardly Roman corporal.*
ROMAN SOLDIERS, *two or more.*

Prologue.

We beg the kind attention and lenient criticism of the audience, while we attempt to perform a little tragic passage from one of the almost forgotten dramas of Beaumont and Fletcher. Our piece is entitled, *Caratach and Hengo;* the scene of action is Britain; the time about 60 A. D. Caratach is another name for Caractacus, whose story is familiar to students of English history. He is represented as a brave general of the Britons, reduced to the last extremity of war, deserted by his soldiers, and hunted, like a wild beast, by the Roman invaders of his native island. His nephew, Hengo, a heroic boy of the royal blood, accompanies Caratach. Hengo's touching fidelity and noble courage are delineated in words worthy of Shakespeare. His patient suffering from hunger, and his cruel death, can not but move the sympathies of those who enter into the spirit of the poem.

We are aware that it is hazardous for amateurs to undertake the representation of tragic scenes; but the simplicity of the action, in our play, and the literary interest of the selection, induce us in this instance to risk the wrath of Melpomene, and your possible censure.

SCENE I:—*A Forest. Enter* CARATACH *and* HENGO. *They pause at* C.

Caratach. How does my boy?
Hengo. I do not fear.
Car. My good boy?
Hengo. I know, uncle,
We must all die; my little brother died,

I saw him die, and he died smiling; sure
There 's no great pain in 't, uncle. But pray tell me
Whither must we go when we 're dead?
Car. Strange questions!
Why to the blessed'st place boy. Ever sweetness
And happiness dwell there.
Hengo. Will you come to me?
Car. Yes, my sweet boy.
Hengo. Mine aunt, too, and my cousins?
Car. All, my good child.
Hengo. No Romans, uncle?
Car. No, boy.
Hengo. I should be loth to meet them there.
Car. No ill men,
That live by violence, and strong oppression,
Come thither; 't is for those the gods love, good men.
Hengo. Why then I care not when I go, for surely
I am persuaded they love me: I never
Blasphemed them, uncle; nor transgressed my parents;
I always said my prayers.
Car. Thou shalt go, then,
Indeed thou shalt.
Hengo. When they please.
Car. That 's my good boy!
Art thou not weary, Hengo?
Hengo. Weary, uncle?
I 've heard you say you 've marched all day in armor.

Car. I have, boy.
Hengo. Am not I your kinsman?
Car. Yes.
Hengo. And am not I as fully allied unto you
In those brave things, as blood?
Car. Thou art too tender.
Hengo. To go upon my legs? They were made to bear me.
I can play twenty miles a day; I see no reason,
But to preserve my country and myself,
I should march forty.
Car. What wouldst thou be, living
To wear a man's strength!
Hengo Why, a Caratach, [*With fire.*
A Roman-hater, a scourge sent from heaven
To whip these proud thieves from our kingdom. Hark! [*Drum.*
Hark, uncle, hark! I hear a drum.
[*Enter at* L. JUDAS *and soldiers.* CARATACH *retires to* R., *shielding* HENGO, *and sternly eyeing soldiers.*
Judas. Beat softly,
Softly, I say; they 're here. Who dares charge?
1st Sol. He,
That dares be knocked o 'the head;
I 'll not come near him.
Judas. Retire again, and watch, then. How he stares!
He has eyes would kill a dragon.
Mark the boy well;
If we could take or kill him. A pox on ye,

How fierce ye look! See how he broods the boy!
The devil dwells in 's scabbard. Back, I say!
Apace, apace! he has found us. [*They retire.*

Car. Do ye hunt us?

Hengo. Uncle, good uncle, see! the thin starved rascal,
The eating Roman, see where he thrids the thickets;
Kill him, dear uncle, kill him!

Car. Do ye make us foxes?—
Here, hold my charging-staff, and keep the place, boy!
I am at bay, and like a bull, I 'll bear me.
Stand, stand, ye rogues, ye squirrels!

[*Draws and rushes after them*, L.

Hengo. Now he pays them;
Oh, that I had a man's strength!

[*Enter at* L. JUDAS.

Judas. Here 's the boy;
Mine own, I thank my fortune.

Hengo. Uncle, uncle!
Famine is fallen upon me, uncle.

Judas. Come, sir,
Yield willingly, your uncle 's out of hearing.

Hengo. I defy thee,
Thou mock-made man of mat: Charge home, sirrah!
Hang thee, base slave, thou shak 'st.

Judas. Upon my conscience,
The boy will beat me! how it looks, how bravely,
How confident the worm is! a scabbed boy
To handle me thus! Yield, or I cut thy head off.

Hengo. Thou darest not cut my finger; here 't is, touch it.

Judas. The boy speaks sword and buckler! Pr'ythee yield, boy;
Come, here 's an apple, yield.

Hengo. [*Aside*] By Heaven, he fears me!
I 'll give you sharper language: When, ye coward,
When come ye up?

Judas. If he should beat me—

Hengo. When, sir?
I long to kill thee! Come, thou
Canst not 'scape me;
I 've twenty ways to charge thee, twenty deaths
Attend my bloody staff.

Judas. Sure, 't is the devil,
A dwarf devil in a doublet!

Hengo. I have killed
A captain, sirrah, a brave captain, and when I've done,
I've kicked him thus. Look here: see how I charge
This staff! [*Threatens to charge.*

Judas. Most certain this boy will cut my throat yet.

[*Enter* R. *two soldiers, running. They rush past* HENGO.

1st Sol. Flee, flee, he kills us.

2d Sol. He comes, he comes!

Judas. The devil take the hindmost!

[*Exeunt* L. JUDAS *and soldiers.*

Hengo. Run, run, ye rogues, ye precious rogues, ye rank rogues!

'A comes, 'a comes, 'a comes, 'a comes! that's he, boys! [*Goes to extreme* L.
What a brave cry they make! [*Enter* CARATACH, R.

Car. How does my chicken?

Hengo. Faith, uncle, grown a soldier, a great soldier; [*Meets* CARATACH *in* C.
For, by the virtue of your charging-staff,
And a strange fighting face I put upon it,
I've out-braved Hunger.

Car. That's my boy, my sweet boy,
Come, chicken, let's go seek some place of strength
(The country's full of scouts) to rest awhile in;
Thou wilt not else be able to endure
The journey to my country. Fruits and water
Must be your food awhile, boy.

Hengo. Any thing;
I can eat moss, nay, I can live on anger,
To vex these Romans. Let's be wary, uncle.

Car. I warrant thee; come cheerfully.

Hengo. And boldly! [*Exeunt,* L.

SCENE II:—*Another part of the forest.* *Enter* MACER *and* JUDAS, (L.)

Macer. What news?

Judas. I've lodged him; rouse him, he that dares.

Macer. Where, Judas?

Judas. On a steep rock i' th' woods, the boy, too, with him;
And there he swears he'll keep his Christmas, Macer,

But he will come away with full conditions,
Bravely, and like a Briton. He paid part of us;
Yet I think we fought bravely: For mine own part,
I was four several times at half-sword with him,
Twice stood his partizan; but the plain truth is,
He's a mere devil, and no man. I' th' end he swinged us,
And swinged us soundly, too; he fights by witchcraft;
Yet for all that I saw him lodged.

Macer. Take more men, and scout him round.
What victuals has he?

Judas. Not a piece of biscuit,
Not so much as will stop a tooth, nor water.
They lie
Just like a brace of bear-whelps, close and crafty,
Sucking their fingers for their food.
His sword by his side, plumbs of a pound weight by him,
Will make your chops ache: You'll find it more labor
To win him living, than climbing of a crow's nest.

Macer. Away, and compass him; we shall come up,
I'm sure, within these two hours. Watch him close.
[*Exit.*

Judas. He shall fly through the air, if he escape me. [*Enter a soldier with meat and a bottle.*

Sol. 'Here, Judas, I have brought the meat and water.'

Judas. Hang it on the side of the rock as though the Britons
Stole hither to relieve him: Who first ventures
To fetch it off is ours. I can not see him.

Sol. He lies close, in a hole above, I know it,
Gnawing upon his anger,—Ha! no; 't is not he.

Judas. Make no noise; if he stir, a deadly tempest
Of huge stones falls upon us.

[*Soldier goes out* R., *leaves provisions behind scene and returns to* JUDAS.

Sol. 'T is done! Away, close! [*Exeunt,* L.

SCENE III:—CARATACH *discovered, with* HENGO *sleeping on the ground.*

Car. Sleep still, sleep sweetly, child; 't is all thou feed'st on.
No gentle Briton near, no valiant charity,
To bring thee food? Poor knave, thou 'rt sick, extreme sick,
Almost grown wild for meat; and yet thy goodness
Will not confess nor show it. All the woods
Are double lined with soldiers; no way left us
To make a noble 'scape. I 'll sit down by thee,
And, when thou wak'st, either get meat to save thee,
Or lose my life i' th' purchase, good gods comfort thee.
The boy begins to stir; thy safety made,
Would my soul were in Heaven.

Hengo. [*Waking*] Oh, noble uncle,
Look out; I dreamed we were betrayed.

Car. No harm, boy;
'T is but thy emptiness that breeds these fancies;
Thou shalt have meat anon.

Hengo. A little, uncle,
And I shall hold out bravely.

[HENGO *rises.* CARATACH *espies the meat and water outside.*

Car. Courage, my boy! I have found meat.
Look, Hengo, [*Joyously.*
Look where some blessed Briton, to preserve thee,
Has hung a little food and drink;
Cheer up, boy;
Do not forsake me now!

Hengo. Oh, uncle, uncle,
I feel I can not stay long; yet I 'll fetch it,
To keep your noble life. Uncle, I 'm heart-whole,
And would live.

Car. Thou shalt, long, I hope.

Hengo. But my head, uncle! Methinks the rock goes round.

[*Enter stealthily* JUDAS, *with bow and arrow*, L.

Do not you hear
The noise of bells?

Car. Of bells, boy? 'T is thy fancy.

Hengo. Methinks, sir,
They ring a strange sad knell, a preparation
To some near funeral of state: Nay, weep not,
Mine own sweet uncle! you will kill me sooner.

Car. Oh, my poor chicken!

Hengo. Fy! faint-hearted uncle?

Car. I 'll go myself, boy.

Hengo. No, as you love me, uncle.
I will not eat it, if I do not fetch it.
The danger only I desire. When I have brought it, uncle,
We 'll be as merry—

Car. Go, i' th' name of Heaven, boy!

Hengo. [*Exit*, R.] I have it.—[JUDAS *shoots*] Oh!

Car. What ail'st thou?

[*Re-enter* HENGO, *with an arrow in his side.*

Hengo. Oh, my best uncle, I am slain!

Car. [*Seeing* JUDAS] I see you,
And Heaven direct my hand!

[JUDAS *steals off* L. CAR. *hurls a stone after him.*

Destruction
Go with thy coward soul! How dost thou, boy?

[*Supports* HENGO.

Hengo. Oh, uncle, uncle,
Oh, how it pricks me—am I preserved for this?—
Extremely pricks me.

Car. Coward, rascal, coward!
Dogs eat thy flesh!

Hengo. Oh, I bleed hard; I faint, too; out upon 't,
How sick I am!—The lean rogue, uncle!

Car. Look, boy;
I 've laid him sure enough.

Hengo. Have you knocked his brains out?

Car. I warrant thee, for stirring more: Cheer up, child.

Hengo. Hold my sides hard; stop, stop; oh, wretched fortune,
Must we part thus? Still I grow sicker, uncle.

Car. Heaven look upon this noble child!

Hengo. I once hoped
I should have lived to have met these bloody Romans
At my sword's point, to have revenged my father,
To have beaten them. Oh, hold me hard! But, uncle—

Car. Thou shalt live still, I hope, boy. Shall I draw it?

Hengo. You draw away my soul, then; I would live
A little longer,—spare me, Heavens!—but only
[*Tries to stand alone.*
To thank you for your tender love. Good uncle,
Good, noble uncle, weep not!

Car. Oh, my chicken,
My dear boy, what shall I lose?

Hengo. Why, a child,
That must have died, however; had this 'scaped me,
Fever or famine—I was born to die, sir.

Car. But thus unblown, my boy?

Hengo. I go the straighter
My journey to the gods. Sure I shall know you
When you come, uncle?

Car. Yes, boy.

Hengo. And I hope
We shall enjoy together that great blessédness
You told me of.

Car. Most certain, child.

Hengo. I grow cold;
Mine eyes are going.

Car. Lift them up.

Hengo. Pray for me;
And, noble uncle, when my bones are ashes,
Think of your little nephew. Mercy!

Car. Mercy!
You blessed angels, take him.

Hengo. Kiss me. So.
Farewell, farewell! [*Dies.*

Car. Farewell the hopes of Britain!
Thou royal graft, farewell forever! Time and death
You 've done your worst. Fortune, now see, now proudly
Pluck off thy veil, and view thy triumph: Look,
Look what thou hast brought this land to. Oh, fair flower,
How lovely yet thy ruins show, how sweetly
Even death embraces thee! The peace of Heaven,
The fellowship of all great souls, be with thee!
[*Mournful music.*

Curtain.

COSTUMES.

Caratach.—Vest and short trowsers of pleated cloth; belt and broad sword; short cloak of Scotch plaid, mostly blue; sandals; conical cap of buckram, covered with checkered cloth; heavy necklace or chain of twisted wires, representing gold and silver; hair in long bushy curls down the back; immense tangled mustaches; circular shield of wicker; heavy charging-staff, or spear.

Hengo.—Flesh-colored legs and arms; beautiful tunic of Scotch plaid; short cloak of same; sandals; bracelets of gold; long black hair; no covering on the head.

Judas.—Close-fitting tunic, belted about the waist, the skirt falling to the knees in folds; flesh arms and legs; sandals; helmet; metallic shield on left arm; spear, (in third scene, bow and arrow); dirk at right side.

Macer.—Coat of mail; helmet; sword.

Soldiers.—Similar to Judas; spears; helmets.

A SURPRISED SUITOR; OR, PHILPOT'S COURTSHIP.

From The Citizen, by Murphy.

PERSONS REPRESENTED.

GEORGE PHILPOT. MARIA.

SCENE I:—*A Parlor.* MARIA *and* GEORGE PHILPOT *discovered.*

Maria. [*Aside*] A pretty sort of a lover they have found for me.

G. Phil. [*Aside*] How shall I speak my mind to her; she is almost a stranger to me.

Maria. [*Aside*] Now, I'll make the hideous thing hate me, if I can.

G. Phil. [*Aside*] Ay, she is as sharp as a needle, I warrant her. Her father says she's a prodigy.

Maria. [*Aside*] When will he begin? [*Peeps at him*] Ah, you fright! I'll give him an aversion to me, that's what I will, and so let him have the trouble of breaking off the match: I'll make believe I'm an idiot,—not a word yet—he is in a fine confusion. [*Looks foolish*] I think I may as well sit down, sir.

G. Phil. Madam, I—I—I—I 'll hand you a chair, madam; there, madam. [*Bows awkwardly.*

Maria. Sir, I thank you.

G. Phil. [*In confusion*] I 'll sit down, too.

Maria. Heigho!

G. Phil. Madam!

Maria. Sir.

G. Phil. I thought—I—I—did not you say something, madam?

Maria. No, sir; nothing.

G. Phil. I beg your pardon, madam.

Maria. [*Aside*] Oh, you are a sweet creature.

G. Phil. [*Aside*] The ice is broken, now; I have begun, and so I'll go on.

[*Sits silent, looks foolish, and steals a look at her.*

Maria. [*Aside*] An agreeable interview, this.

G. Phil. Pray, madam, do you ever go to concerts?

Maria. Concerts! What 's that, sir?

G. Phil. A music meeting.

Maria. I have been at a Quaker's meeting, but never at a music meeting.

G. Phil. Oh, madam, all the gay world goes to concerts. The notable! [*Aside*] I 'll take courage, she is nobody. Will you give me leave to present you a ticket, madam?

Maria. [*Looking simple and awkward*] A ticket! What is a ticket?

G. Phil. There, madam, at your service.

[*Gives a card.*

Maria. [*Curtsies awkwardly*] I long to see what a ticket is.

G. Phil. [*Aside*] What a curtsey there is for the St. James end of town! I hate her; she seems to be an idiot.

Maria. [*Aside*] Here 's a charming ticket he has given me. And is this a ticket, sir?

G. Phil. Yes, madam. [*Mimicks her aside*] And is this a ticket?

Maria. [*Reads*] *For sale, the following goods—thirty chests, straw hats; fifty tubs, chip hats; pepper, sago, borax*—Ha, ha! such a ticket!

G. Phil. I—I—I have made a mistake, madam—here, here is the right one.

Maria. You need not mind it, sir; I never go to such places.

G. Phil. No, madam? [*Aside*] I do n't know what to make of her.

Maria. [*Aside*] A pretty husband my papa has chosen for me!

G. Phil. [*Aside*] What shall I say to her next? Have you been at the burletta, madam?

Maria. Where?

G. Phil. The burletta.

Maria. Sir, I would have you to know that I am no such person. I go to burlettas! I am not what you take me for.

G. Phil. Madam—

Maria. I am come of good people, sir; and have been properly educated, as a young girl ought to be.

G. Phil. [*Aside*] What a fool she is! The burletta is an opera, madam.

Maria. Opera, sir! I do n't know what you mean by this usage—to affront me in this manner!

G. Phil. Affront! I mean quite the reverse, madam, I took you for a connoisseur.

Maria. Who, me a connoisseur, sir! I desire you won't call me such names. I am sure I never so much as thought of such a thing. Sir, I won't be called a connoisseur—I won't—I won't—I won't.

[*Bursts out crying.*

G. Phil. Madam, I meant no offense. A connoisseur is a virtuoso.

Maria. Do n't virtuoso me! I am no virtuoso, sir.

G. Phil. But, madam, you mistake me, quite. [*Aside*] The girl 's a natural—so much the better,—I 'll marry her and lock her up. Madam, upon my word, you misunderstand me.

Maria. [*Drying her eyes*] I won't be called a connoisseur, by you or any body, and I won't be called a virtuoso either—I would have you to know that, sir.

G. Phil. Madam, connoisseur and virtuoso are words for a person of taste.

Maria. Taste!

G. Phil. Yes, madam.

Maria. And did you mean to say as how I am a person of taste?

G. Phil. Undoubtedly.

Maria. Sir, your most obedient humble servant. Oh, that 's another thing. I have a taste, to be sure.

G. Phil. I know you have, madam—[*Aside*] Oh, you 're a precious ninny!

Maria. Yes, I know I have; I can read tolerably, and I begin to write a little.

G. Phil. Upon my word, you have made a great progress! [*Aside*] What could Old Square-toes mean, by passing her upon me for a sensible girl? And what a fool I was to be afraid to speak to her! I 'll talk to her openly at once. Pray, madam, are you inclined to matrimony?

Maria. Yes, sir.

G. Phil. How should you like me?

Maria. Of all things—

G. Phil. [*Aside*] A girl without ceremony. Do you love me?

Maria. Yes, sir.

G. Phil. But you do n't love any body else?

Maria. Yes, sir.

G. Phil. [*Aside*] Frank and free. But not so well as me?

Maria. Yes, sir.

G. Phil. Better, may be?

Maria. Yes, sir.

G. Phil. You do!

Maria. Yes, sir.

G. Phil. The case is clear; Miss Maria, your very humble servant; you are not for my money, I promise you.

Maria. Sir!

G. Phil. I have done, madam, that 's all; and I take my leave.

Maria. But you 'll marry me?

G. Phil. No, madam, no; no such thing—you may provide yourself a husband elsewhere: I am your humble servant.

Maria. Not marry me, Mr. Philpot? But you must—My papa said you must—and I will have you.

G. Phil. [*Aside*] There 's another proof of her nonsense. Make yourself easy, I shall have nothing to do with you.

Maria. Not marry me, Mr. Philpot? [*Bursts into tears*] But I say you shall; and I will have a husband, or I 'll know the reason why—You shall,—you shall.

G. Phil. A pretty sort of a wife they intend for me, here—

Maria. I wonder you a' n't ashamed of yourself, to affront a young girl in this manner. I 'll go and tell my papa—I will—I will—I will.

[*Crying bitterly.*

G. Phil. And so you may—I have no more to say to you—And so, your servant, miss,—your servant.

Maria. Ay! and my brother Bob shall fight you.

G. Phil. What care I for your brother Bob?

[*Going.*

Maria. How can you be so cruel, Mr. Philpot? how can you—Oh! [*Cries and struggles with him.*

Exit G. PHILPOT] Ha! ha! I have carried my brother's scheme into execution, charmingly, ha, ha! He will break off the match now of his own accord, ha, ha! This is charming! this is fine! this is like a girl of spirit. [*Exit.*

SCENE II:—*The same. Enter* MARIA, *and* G. PHILPOT, *dressed foppishly.*

G. Phil. I know she is a fool, and so I will speak to her without ceremony.—Well, miss, you told me you could read and write.

Maria. Read, sir? Gracious! [*Looking at him*] Ha, ha, ha!

G. Phil. What does she laugh at?

Maria. Ha, ha, ha, ha!

G. Phil. What diverts you so, pray?

Maria. Ha, ha, ha! What a fine tawdry figure you have made of yourself! Ha, ha!

G. Phil. Figure, madam!

Maria. I shall die, I shall die! Ha, ha, ha!

G. Phil. Do you make a laughing-stock of me?

Maria. No, sir; by no means—Ha, ha, ha!

G. Phil. Let me tell you, miss, I do n't understand being treated thus.

Maria. Sir, I can't possibly help it—I—I—Ha, ha!

G. Phil. I shall quit the room, and tell your papa, if you go on thus.

Maria. Sir, I beg your pardon a thousand times

—I am but a giddy girl—I can't help it—I—I—Ha, ha!

G. Phil. Madam, this is downright insult!

Maria. Sir, you look somehow or other—I do n't know how, so comically—Ha, ha, ha!

G. Phil. Now, here is an idiot in spirits—I tell you, this is your ignorance—I am dressed in high taste.

Maria. Yes; so you are—Ha, ha, ha!

G. Phil. Will you have done laughing?

Maria. Yes, sir, I will—I will—there—there—there—I have done. [*Aside*] I won't look at him, and then I sha' n't laugh—

G. Phil. Let me tell you, miss, that nobody understands dress better than I do.

Maria. Ha, ha, ha!

G. Phil. She 's mad, sure!

Maria. No, sir, I am not mad—I have done, sir, —I have done—I assure you, sir, that nobody is more averse from ill-manners, and would take greater pains not to affront a gentleman—[*Glancing at him*] Ha, ha, ha!

G. Phil. Again? Zounds! what do you mean? you 'll put me in a passion, I can tell you, presently.

Maria. I can't help it—indeed, I can't help it. Ha, ha, ha!

G. Phil. I never met with such usage in my life.

Maria. I shall die! Do, sir, let me laugh—It will do me good—Ha, ha, ha!

[*Sits down in a fit of laughing.*

G. Phil. If this is your way, I won't stay a minute longer in the room—I'll go this moment and tell your father.

Maria. Sir, sir, Mr. Philpot, do n't be so hasty, sir, I have done, sir; it 's over now—I have had my laugh out—I am a giddy girl—but I 'll be grave.—[*Aside*] I 'll compose myself, and act a different scene with him from what I did in the morning. I have all the materials of an impertinent wit, and I will now twirl him about the room, like a boy setting up his top with his finger and thumb.

G. Phil. Miss, I think you told me you could read and write?

Maria. Read, sir! Reading is the delight of my life—I do love reading, sir! Do you love reading, sir?

G. Phil. Prodigiously—[*Aside*] How pert she is grown!—I have read very little, and I 'm resolved, for the future, to read less. What have you read, miss?

Maria. Every thing.

G. Phil. You have?

Maria. Yes, sir, I have read every thing: Suckling, Waller, Milton, Dryden, Lansdowne, Gay, Prior, Swift, Addison, Pope, Young, Thompson.

G. Phil. Hey!—what a clack is here!

[*He walks across the stage.*

Maria. [*Following him eagerly*] Shakespeare, Fletcher, Otway, Southerne, Rowe, Congreve, Wicherly, Farquhar, Cibber, Vanbrugh, Steele, in short, every body ; and I find them all wit, fire, vivacity, spirit, genius, taste, imagination, raillery, humor, character, and sentiment. [*Aside*] Well done, Miss Notable! You have played your part like a young actress in high favor with the town.

G. Phil. Her tongue goes like a water-mill.

Maria. What 's the matter, sir. Why, you look as if the stocks were fallen—or like a politician without news; or like a prude without scandal; or like a great lawyer without a brief; or like some lawyers with one—or—

G. Phil. Or like a poor dupe of a husband hen-pecked by a wit, and so no more of that. [*Aside*] What a capricious piece here is!

Maria. Oh, fie! you have spoiled all, I had not half done!

G. Phil. There is enough of all conscience. You may content yourself.

Maria. But I can't be so easily contented—I like a simile half a mile long.

G. Phil. I see you do.

Maria. Oh! And I make verses, too,—verses like an angel—off hand—*extempore.* Can you give me an *extempore?*

G. Phil. What does she mean? No, miss, I have never one about me.

Maria. You can't give me an *extempore*—Oh! for shame, Mr. Philpot! I love an *extempore* of all things; and I love the poets dearly; their sense so fine, their invention rich as Pactolus.

G. Phil. A poet rich as Pactolus! I have heard of that Pactolus in the city.

Maria. Very like.

G. Phil. But you never heard of a poet as rich as he.

Maria. As who?

G. Phil. Pactolus.—He was a great Jew merchant—

Maria. Pactolus a Jew merchant! Pactolus is a river.

G. Phil. A river!

Maria. Yes—don't you understand geography?

G. Phil. The girl 's crazy!

Maria. Oh! sir, if you don't understand geography, you are nobody. I understand geography, and I understand orthography; you know I told you I can write—and I can dance, too—will you dance a minuet? [*Sings and dances.*

G. Phil. You sha' n't lead me a dance, I promise you.

Maria. Oh! very well, sir—you refuse me—remember you 'll hear immediately of my being married to another, and then you 'll be ready to hang yourself.

G. Phil. Not I, I promise you.

Maria. Oh! very well, very well—remember—mark my words. I 'll do it, you shall see—Ha, ha! [*Runs off in a fit of laughing.*

G. Phil. Marry her! No, no! I 'll have nothing to do with her. [*Exit.*

THE LOVES OF MISS TUCKER.

From Douglas Jerrold's Time Works Wonders.

PERSONS REPRESENTED.

Miss Tucker.	Bessy Tulip.
Florentine.	Professor Truffles.
Chicken, *a maid servant.*	Bantam, *a footman.*

Scene I:—*A Wood Path. Enter* Miss Tucker, *and* Florentine *with a portfolio.*

Floren. Ha! ha! How often have I heard you wish you had been born a huntress! And now—in this blessed month of June, you 'd sit by the fireside, and do nothing but grow roses in worsted. Keep house such an hour as this! Why, 't is treason to nature.

Miss T. Allow me to observe—though, as I 'm a dependent, I know I have no right to speak—that your frequent allusions to nature are not decorous. With young women of my time, nature was the last thing thought of. I know I 'm only a dependent; and people who live in other people's houses should have no tongues,—no eyes,—no—

Floren. I can not bear this—I will not bear it. You hurt me—wound me deeply. If it irk you to dwell beneath the same roof—if it constrain you in the least, though why it should, I know not—choose your own abode; share my little fortune, how and where you will. But I can not have my friendship taken as alms; my love thus ever chilled by the cold sense of obligation. You have at length forced me to speak. It is unkind of you—indelicate.

Miss T. Indelicate! Such a word to me—to me, who have kept parlor boarders. I know I 'm only an interloper; but can gratitude be indelicate?

Floren. It may be mean. True gratitude, in very fullness of its soul, knows not the limits of its debt: but when it weighs each little gift—books down each passing courtesy—it ceases to be gratitude, and sinks to calculation. Why, I hope I am grateful for the flowers at my feet, but I were most unworthy of their sweetness, could I coldly sit me down to count them. I entreat you, no more of this.

Miss T. You know I love you,—always loved you more than the other girls: for when they were all at their romps, did n't I always lock you up that you might be safe? And I 'm sure you 're very kind now. I have, I know, the best bedroom—though yours, no doubt, will be the warmest in winter. I have the best side of the fire-place, but then it 's not my own fire-place; and, as for gifts, it was very kind of you a week ago to give me this gown, though if I 'd gone to the mercer's with my own money, 't is the very last color I should have thought of.

Floren. The fault was in my eyes; next week you shall choose for yourself.

Miss T. I dreamt on Friday of a black satin; but Friday's dreams seldom come true; and then 't is impertinent in poor people to dream at any time beyond their means.

Floren. Nay, it shall be your privilege to dream, and mine to turn your visions to realities. Now, like a dear, good governess, for still you are so,—come with me, that I may finish my sketch of that beautiful oak.

Miss T. Why look at the clouds—I 'm sure there 'll be a storm, and you might have finished it on Tuesday.

Floren. You know we were interrupted.

Miss T. Interrupted! What, because a gentleman stood to stare at you? You should have let him stare—have never seen him—but have gone on the harder showing your accomplishments. When a young woman can't do this, the blessings of education are lost upon her.

Floren. Never fear; I shall be hardened in time. Now, only half an hour; this is the path.

Miss T. Ha! the last time we trod that path, *he* was with us, and where, where is he now?

Floren. In a beautiful glass case—yes, shrined in crystal, as such a creature ought to be.

Miss T. He was the pearl of pugs. But it has ever been *my* fate! As the sweetest of poets sings—

"I never reared a young gazelle
To glad me with its soft black eye,
But when it came to know me well,—
And love me, it was sure to die!"

Floren. There certainly was a sentiment about that dog!

Miss T. He could n't move for sentiment. I see him now—with his beautiful face, so black, yet so benignant! Now cropping a daisy with his lily-white teeth; and now looking up and barking at me, as if he knew my inmost thoughts—

Floren. And quite agreed with them.

Miss T. But he is dead—murdered!

Floren. Compose yourself: I'll buy a parrot, warranted to live a hundred years; so that you may both descend to your peaceful graves together.

Miss T. Florentine, the human heart is not a peg, now to hang one thing upon, and now another.

And people who live in other people's houses have no right to the use of their own affections: though, to be sure, but for the conduct of some people, [*meaning* FLORENTINE] I might still have a house of my own. Oh, I forgive you: but that bold minx, Miss Bessy Tulip—

Floren. Dear, dear Bessy! And she is now in India.

Miss T. I hope they'll carry her a million miles up the country, and marry her to a blackamoor.

Floren. She ought to marry an Indian king.

Miss T. A king! a king with a ring in his nose. Ugh! you never knew her arts: a little lapwing! I've caught her with—ha! I forget his name; but I've seen her leering and looking, and sidling round him, like a kitten round a cream jug.

Floren. Ha! ha! Bless her merry heart! and she was good as she was merry: for she had n't a thought but she spoke it.

Miss T. The more shame for her. In my time, girls would have blushed to do such a thing. But for her boldness, you'd never have run away with the baronet's nephew.

Floren. Nay, we shall lose this most delicious light.

Miss T. But you have very properly picked him from your heart, like a crooked letter from a sampler.

Floren. Sure 't was an easy task for five long years; and there 's not a day I have n't worked at it. Come.

Miss T. [*Embracing her*] Thus, my dear girl, like two roses on an uninhabited island, we 'll live and die a death of natural sweetness. And for Clarence Norman—

Floren. And for Juba, the pug!

Miss T. Florentine, this is cruel. I—positively I can not follow you: I see him move in every shadow, hear him bark in every bush.

Floren. Then I 'll go alone.

Miss T. Impossible. Whatever be my feelings, I 'll struggle as I walk; and you said something about a parrot? I think I could love—but then it must be a gray parrot.

Floren. It shall be as gray as old Time.

Miss T. For I 've nobody but you in the world, and the heart, the heart—must love something.

[*Exeunt.*

SCENE II:—FLORENTINE'S *House. Enter* BESSY *and* MISS TUCKER.

Bessy. Well, if you had n't such a strong mind, and hated all such nonsense, I vow I should think you in love.

Miss T. *I* in love!

Bessy. Yes, for they say love 's like the measles: all the worse when it comes late in life.

Miss T. Late in life! child!

Bessy. Oh, did n't I see you last night! When Professor Truffles came suddenly before you, did n't you turn red and white, and white and red. I could n't have done it better myself at sixteen.

Miss T. Do n't confound emotions, girl. You do n't know what I 'd suffered from the thunder. It 's well enough for you with nerves like fiddle-strings; but you do n't know my fragility. I have n't winked an eye this blessed night.

Bessy. Well, you *do* look a little foggy, that 's the truth.

Miss T. Foggy, miss! I beg your pardon,—mistress, and mistress what? I suppose your husband gave you a name.

Bessy. Oh! you shall hear that when my husband comes. Call me Bessy; it takes me back to that blissful time when you used to carve thin slices for us. But what can make Flory so late?

Miss T. Dear girl! her sensibility. The baronet has offered her his heart, and—

Bessy. And what of that?

Miss T. She 's flurried, of course, as a gentlewoman ought to be. Would you have a woman take a man's heart as though it was a sandwich?

Bessy. Why that 's quite according to the appetite she may have for it.

Miss T. Appetite! Was there ever such an expression? Positively you make me quite shudder.

Bessy. Offered his heart! And Flory is at once to be Lady Norman? Umph! And I suppose you 'll live with her at the fine mansion?

Miss T. If she forcibly insists upon it—not but

what it's very miserable living in other people's houses. [*Aside*] There's a crimson and gold room, with a southern look, that I already see my tambour-frame in.

Bessy. Marry the baronet! And she's quite forgotten his poor nephew?

Miss T. They've forgotten one another; and now laugh at their love with a common sense that's quite delightful.

Bessy. [*Aside*] I'm not so sure of that.

[*Enter* CHICKEN.

Chick. Professor Truffles, ma'am.

Miss T. Who?

Chick. Professor Truffles. I did n't know him at first. He used to be as rusty as old iron, and now, la! he's as fine as if he'd been black-leaded.

Miss T. Show him in—no, yes. [*To* BESSY] You'll not leave me?

Bessy. Never. [*Aside*] I'll stop and see the fun.

Chick. I left him looking at the pug in the glass-case; the pug he gave you. He seemed quite affected. [*Exit.*

Miss T. [*Aside*] Thank Heaven he has some fellow feeling left! [*To* BESSY] You're sure you'll not leave me?

Bessy. Never—never. Dear me! How you tremble; why it's only the professor. There's no thunder in him, you know. [*Enter* TRUFFLES.

Truffles. Madam,—Miss Tucker.— [*Aside*] My tongue tastes like brass in my mouth; and for the first time brass, I can make little of. Madam, seven variegated years have passed since in friendly conference we met.

Miss T. Is it so long, sir?

Truff. Yes, madam, I can look at you and say full seven years. You may remember this watch?

[*Producing it.*

Bessy. Oh, as a child I 've seen the inside of it a thousand times. It 's jeweled, and goes upon what they call a—a duplicate movement.

Truff. [*Aside*] It has gone so once or twice.

Miss T. Well, sir?

Truff. I have in vain, madam, sought you to return it to you. Every year I have hoarded this repeater with—I may say—growing interest.

Miss T. [*Aside*] Ha! the same honey in his syllables.

Truff. It brought you hourly to my mind.

Miss T. [*Aside*] I shall forgive him all.

Truff. For, like you, it was of precious workmanship—

Bessy. [*Aside*] And, like her, as I remember, striking every quarter. [*Retires.*

Truff. And, like you, it—it—[*aside*] it bore the marks of time upon its face. Take it, madam, and if it went upon a thousand jewels, let it go upon a thousand and one, and hang it at your heart.

Miss T. Oh! sir, I—I feel I ought not to take it.

Truff. [*Aside*] I feel so, too, but I know she will. [*She takes it*] I said so.

Miss T. Seven years! Can it be seven years?

Truff. Every minute of it: you may trust the watch—it keeps time like a tax-gatherer. [*Aside*] That ugly business well off my hands, and luckily before a witness, too, I feel so honest that I'll swagger.

Miss T. Seven years! Both our hearts have had many thoughts since then. When we last met, professor—

Truff. When we last met, ma'am, my heart was like a summer walnut, green and tender; now I can tell you it's plaguy hard in the shell.

Miss T. [*Aside*] Hard in the shell! Would he freeze my tenderness? Oh, that I could laugh like Florentine! Ha! ha! no doubt. Hard, shrivelled, moldy, and not worth the cracking,—I've known 'em so.

Truff. Very true, ma'am; not to be eaten by any woman,—with salt, or without it. A glorious safety!

Miss T. [*Aside*] His every word's a Whitechapel needle to my soul—but he shall not see it. Ha! ha! ha! to be sure. We *do* change. What we rather like one time we abominate another.

Truff. Yes; for the things themselves change so too. Now, I'm fond, very fond of nice, plump, ripe grapes; but I can't abide 'em when they're shrivelled into raisins.

Miss T. Raisins! [*Aside*] He means me. Ha! ha! ha! [*Aside*] I shall end in a spasm. Bessy,—

[*she runs down*] nothing. You should only hear the professor—so droll,—ha! ha! so very, very droll.

Bessy. [*Aside to her*] Do n't laugh in that way: it 's cruel. It 's punishing nature, and only for wanting to cry.

Miss T. Cry! I shall expire with enjoyment. Oh, you—you witty man. No,—not another word. Thank you, sir, for my repeater. 'T is at your hands an unlooked for blessing! Not a word, I pray. Raisins! ha! ha! ha! [*Aside*] The walnut-hearted barbarian. Raisins!

[*Exeunt* BESSY *and* MISS TUCKER.

Truff. Hem! Strange is the love of woman: it 's like one's beard; the closer one cuts it the stronger it grows: and both a plague. She has no money, and I can't afford to go gratis. Well, if she should break her heart, I think I could survive the calamity. That watch has been ticking seven years at my conscience. 'T is gone: I can now without qualms look at a church clock and a policeman. [*Exit.*

SCENE III:—*An Apartment in* FLORENTINE'S *House. Enter* BESSY *and* MISS TUCKER.

Bessy. No, we do n't want you either to plot or conspire. All we want is your silence.

Miss T. My silence! That one woman should ask such a thing of another

Bessy. His mother knows we are married, and is

glad of it—and she says she knows his father is to be wheedled.

Miss T. Wheedled! Wheedle a husband! You bring pretty principles into the marriage state. Where did you pick 'em up?

Bessy. In the marriage state, of course, like every other wife. Bless you! when you're married you'll wheedle, too. You can't help it.

Miss T. I should despise myself. No, I should trust to pure reason. Wheedle a husband! Why what is it but to pick the lock of a man's heart with a false key?

Bessy. Well, and if the heart's your own property, there's no felony in that.

[*Enter* CHICKEN, *showing in* BANTAM, *who bears a bouquet and letter.*

Chick. Mr. Bantam, ma'am, from Parsnip Hall. [*Aside to him*] Behave yourself, and don't laugh.

Ban. [*To* BESSY] A letter from Mrs. Goldthumb, for you, ma'am. [*Aside*] I won't laugh if I can help it. [*To* MISS T.] A nosegay from Professor Truffles, for you, ma'am.

Miss T. Impossible!

Ban. So I should have thought—but here it is, ma'am, for all that.

Miss T. Stay without; there may be an answer.

Ban. [*Aside to* CHICKEN] I say, 't is plain that some flowers, like some Christians, come to an untimely end; else nobody would send a nosegay to Miss Tucker. [*Exeunt* BANTAM *and* CHICKEN.

Bessy. Why, what a superb bouquet!

Miss T. An odoriferous compliment from the Professor! There may be a letter in it. No! [*Sighing deeply*] No.

Bessy. Yes, there is—I see it!

Miss T. Where?

Bessy. [*Takes bouquet*] See. In the Indies they send love letters made of nothing but flowers. Now the Professor, who knows every thing, knows this; and this is his letter.

Miss T. Oh, that I could read it!

Bessy. When I was abroad, a Persian lady taught me all about it. Bless you! I can read this like print.

Miss T. Sweet girl! Read, read.

Bessy. [*Aside*] I will—and such an epistle! See. Here 's love-lies-a-bleeding; that 's the Professor. And this big cabbage-rose, blushing upon him; that 's you.

Miss T. Beautiful allegory!

Bessy. Here 's poppies; they mean he can't sleep without thinking of you. Here 's the periwinkle; that means contentment with a little. Here 's a bit of broom; that hints at domestic love.

Miss T. Broom! The hint might have been prettier.

Bessy. Here 's the devil-in-a-bush; that means the cruel fate that has separated you. Here 's rosemary; that 's for the dead pug. Here 's lilies; that 's hope, close to London pride.

Miss T. And what does London pride mean?

Bessy. That means a house in a square, and the best pew in the church. And here, backing the whole, is dragon's mouth.

Miss T. And what does that imply?

Bessy. Dragon's mouth has only one meaning, and that is marriage.

Miss T. Well, you have read it beautifully.

Bessy. Well, you must answer this letter in its own way.

Miss T. Impossible. I know nothing of this sweet science.

Bessy. 'T is only to send exactly the same flowers back, to show you reciprocate his passion.

Miss T. But if I do n't reciprocate.

Bessy. Return him a bunch of bachelor's buttons and there 's an end of it.

Miss T. No. I 'll—ha! ha!—I 'll have some sport with him. [*Enter* CHICKEN.

Chick. 'Professor Truffles, ladies.'

Bessy. 'Ah, the gentleman himself. You may now answer him directly, without any flowers except flowers of speech.'

Miss T. 'Pray do not leave me alone with a gentleman.'

Bessy. 'Two is company, you know.'

[*Exit* BESSY *and* CHICKEN. *Enter* TRUFFLES, *with a rose in his button-hole.*

Truff. 'Pardon the abruptness of my visit. Among the roses, I see. Sweets to the sweet.'

Miss T. 'Flatterer!' [*Playing with bouquet.*

Truff. Beautiful flowers! Allow me. [*Takes the flowers from her*] So delicate, so bright, so odoriferous!—your heart must be among them. I'll wear it next my own!

[*Puts bouquet awkwardly to his bosom.*

Miss T. [*Aside*] Gorgeous man!

Truff. And Florentine marries the baronet?

Miss T. She does him that honor.

Truff. Heigho! And will you reside with her new ladyship?

Miss T. She can't live without me. The whole mansion will be at my disposal. Carriages, servants, every thing. But then, Professor, it 's not one's own mansion; not one's own carriage. And people who live in other people's houses—you understand?

[*Sighing.*

Truff. Perfectly! [*Aside*] I 've so often tried the experiment. I know the girl will give her something handsome to get rid of her; so I'll risk the knot. [*Giving back bouquet*] Ha! 't is sweet, indeed, to call a sweet thing one's own. Charming Tucker, may I call you my own?

Miss T. Truffles!

Truff. As we can do nothing else, we'll follow the fashion, and set up a school apiece. Think of the delight. Our own house—own hearth—own tea-kettle—our own cat!

Miss T. Whither would you lead me? I—I can answer nothing.

Truff. Then let that rose—your fittest representative—answer for you.

Miss T. [*Tremulously taking a rose from her bouquet, and giving it*] Take it—it is myself.

Truff. [*Taking the rose from his lapel, and presenting it*] And this is me!

[*Enter, unobserved,* FLORENTINE *and* BESSY, *on one side, and* BANTAM *and* CHICKEN *on the other.*

Miss T. Is it too late to take it back again?

Truff. It is impounded by Hymen; and again to take it would be to rob the church.

[MISS TUCKER, *seeing* FLORENTINE, *screams, and then deliberately faints, supported by* TRUFFLES.

Tableau.

THE CHAGRINED AUTHOR.

From The Critic, by Sheridan.

PERSONS REPRESENTED.

Sir Fretful Plagiary.	Mr. Dangle.
Mrs. Dangle.	Mr. Sneer.

Servant.

Scene:—Dangle's *House.* Mr. Dangle, Mrs. Dangle, *and* Sneer *discovered sitting near a table.* Dangle *has a newspaper. Enter* Servant, L.

Serv. Sir Fretful Plagiary, sir.

Dan. Beg him to walk up. [*Exit* Servant, L.] Now, Mrs. Dangle, Sir Fretful Plagiary is an author to your own taste.

Mrs. D. I confess he is a favorite of mine, because every body else abuses him.

Sneer. Very much to the credit of your charity, madam, if not of your judgment.

Dan. But, egad, he allows no merit to any author but himself, that 's the truth on 't—though he 's my friend.

Sneer. Never. He is as envious as an old maid verging on the desperation of six-and-thirty.

Dan. Very true, egad—though he 's my friend.

Sneer. Then his affected contempt of all newspaper strictures; though, at he same time, he is the sorest man alive, and shrinks, like scorched parchment, from the fiery ordeal of true criticism.

Dan. There 's no denying it—though he is my friend.

Sneer. You have read the tragedy he has just finished, have n't you?

Dan. Oh, yes; he sent it to me yesterday.

Sneer. Well, and you think it execrable, do n't you?

Dan. Why, between ourselves, egad, I must own—though he 's my friend—that it is one of the most—[*Aside*] he 's here—finished and most admirable perform—

Sir F. [*Without,* L.] Mr. Sneer with him, did you say?

[*Enter* SIR FRETFUL, L. *He crosses to* L. C.

Dan. Ah, my dear friend!—Egad, we were just speaking of your tragedy.—Admirable, Sir Fretful, admirable!

Sneer. (R. C.) You never did any thing beyond it Sir Fretful—never in your life.

Sir F. (L. C.) You make me extremely happy; for without a compliment, my dear Sneer, there is n't a man in the world whose judgment I value as I do yours—and Mr. Dangle's.

Mrs. D. (R.) They are only laughing at you, Sir Fretful, for it was but just now that—

Dan. (L.) Mrs. Dangle! Ah, Sir Fretful, you

know Mrs. Dangle. My friend, Sneer, was rallying just now—He knows how she admires you, and—

Sir F. Oh, Lord, I am sure Mr. Sneer has more taste and sincerity than to—[*Aside*] A despicable double-faced fellow!

Dan. Yes, yes—Sneer will jest—but a better humored—

Sir F. Oh, I know—

Dan. He has a ready turn for ridicule—his wit costs him nothing.

Sir F. [*Aside*] No, egad—or I should wonder how he came by it.

Mrs. D. [*Aside*] Because his jest is always at the expense of his friend.

Dan. But, Sir Fretful, have you sent your play to the managers yet? or can I be of any service to you?

Sir F. [*Pompously*] No, no, I thank you; I sent it to the manager of Covent Garden Theatre this morning.

Sneer. I should have thought, now, that it might have been cast, as the actors call it, better at Drury Lane.

Sir F. Oh, lud! no—never send a play there while I live—harkee! [*Whispers to* SNEER.

Sneer. Writes himself! I know he does—

Sir F. I say nothing—I take away from no man's merit—am hurt at no man's good fortune—I say nothing.—But this I will say—through all my knowledge of life, I have observed—that there is not a passion so strongly rooted in the human heart as envy!

Sneer. I believe you have reason for what you say, indeed.

Sir F. Besides—I can tell you it is not always so safe to leave a play in the hands of those who write themselves.

Sneer. What, they may steal from them, hey, my dear Plagiary?

Sir F. Steal!—to be sure they may; and, egad, serve your best thoughts as gipsies do stolen children—disfigure them to make 'em pass for their own.

Sneer. But your present work is a sacrifice to Melpomene, and he, you know, never—

Sir F. That's no security. A dexterous plagiarist may do any thing.—Why, sir, for aught I know, he might take out some of the best things in my tragedy, and put them into his own comedy.

Sneer. That might be done, I dare be sworn.

Sir F. And then, if such a person gives you the least hint or assistance, he is devilish apt to take the merit of the whole—

Dan. If it succeeds.

Sir F. Aye—but with regard to this piece, I think I can hit that gentleman, for I can safely swear he never read it.

Sneer. I'll tell you how you may hurt him more—

Sir F. How?

Sneer. Swear he wrote it.

Sir F. Plague on 't now, Sneer, I shall take it ill. I believe you want to take away my character as an author!

Sneer. Then I am sure you ought to be very much obliged to me.

Sir F. Hey!—Sir!

Dan. Oh, you know, he never means what he says.

Sir F. Sincerely, then—you do like the piece?

Sneer. Wonderfully!

Sir F. But come, now, there must be something that you think might be mended, hey?—Mr. Dangle, has nothing struck you?

Dan. Why, faith, it is but an ungracious thing, for the most part, to—

Sir F. With most authors it is just so, indeed; they are in general strangely tenacious!—But, for my part, I am never so well pleased as when a judicious critic points out any defect to me; for what is the purpose of showing a work to a friend, if you do n't mean to profit by his opinion?

Sneer. Very true. Why, then, though I seriously admire the piece upon the whole, yet there is one small objection, which, if you 'll give me leave, I 'll mention.

Sir F. Sir, you can't oblige me more.

Sneer. I think it wants incident.

Sir F. Good Heavens!—you surprise me!—wants incident!

Sneer. Yes; I think the incidents are too few.

Sir F. Good Heavens!—Believe me, Mr. Sneer, there is no person for whose judgment I have a more implicit deference. But I protest to you, Mr. Sneer, I am only apprehensive that the incidents are too crowded. My dear Dangle, how does it strike you?

Dan. Really, I can't agree with my friend Sneer. I think the plot quite sufficient; and the first four acts by many degrees the best I ever read or saw in my life. If I might venture to suggest any thing, it is that the interest rather falls off in the fifth.

Sir F. Rises, I believe you mean, sir—

Dan. No; I do n't, upon my word.

Sir F. Yes, yes, you do, upon my soul—it certainly do n't fall off, I assure you.—No, no, it do n't fall off.

Dan. Now, Mrs. Dangle, did n't you say it struck you in the same light?

Mrs. D. (R.) No, indeed, I did not—I did not see a fault in any part of the play from the beginning to the end.

Sir F. [*Crossing to* MRS. DANGLE] Upon my soul, the women are the best judges after all!

Mrs. D. Or, if I made any objection, I am sure it was to nothing in the piece! but that I was afraid it was, on the whole, a little too long.

Sir F. Pray, madam, do you speak as to duration of time; or do you mean that the story is tediously spun out?

Mrs. D. Oh, lud! no. I speak only with reference to the usual length of acting plays.

Sir F. Then I am very happy—very happy, indeed—because the play is a short play, a remarkably short play: I should not venture to differ with a lady on a point of taste; but, on these occasions, the watch, you know, is the critic.

Mrs. D. Then, I suppose, it must have been Mr. Dangle's drawling manner of reading it to me.

Sir F. [*Crosses,* L., *and back to* R. C.] Oh, if Mr. Dangle read it, that's quite another affair! But I assure you, Mrs. Dangle, the first evening you can spare me three hours and a half, I'll undertake to read you the whole, from beginning to end, with the prologue and epilogue, and allow time for the music between the acts.

Mrs. D. I hope to see it on the stage next.

[*Exit,* R.

Dan. Well, Sir Fretful, I wish you may be able to get rid as easily of the newspaper criticisms as you do of ours.

Sir F. [*Crosses,* C.] The newspapers!—Sir, they are the most villainous—licentious—abominable—infernal—Not that I ever read them! no! I make it a rule never to look into a newspaper.

Dan. (L.) You are quite right—for it certainly must hurt an author of delicate feelings to see the liberties they take.

Sir F. No!—quite the contrary; their abuse is, in fact, the best panegyric—I like it, of all things. An author's reputation is only in danger from their support.

Sneer. (R.) Why, that's true—and that attack now on you the other day—

Sir F. What? where?

Dan. Aye, you mean in a paper of Thursday; it was completely ill-natured, to be sure.

Sir F. Oh, so much the better—Ha! ha! ha!—I would n't have it otherwise.

Dan. Certainly, it is only to be laughed at; for—

Sir F. You do n't happen to recollect what the fellow said, do you?

Sneer. Pray, Dangle—Sir Fretful seems a little anxious!

Sir F. Oh, lud, no!—anxious—not I—not the least. I—But one may as well hear, you know.

Dan. Sneer, do you recollect?—[*Aside to* SNEER] Make out something.

Sneer. [*Aside to* DANGLE] I will. [*Aloud*] Yes, yes, I remember perfectly.

Sir F. Well, and pray, now—not that it signifies, what might the gentleman say?

Sneer. Why, he roundly asserts that you have not the slightest invention or original genius whatever; though you are the greatest traducer of all other authors living.

Sir F. Ha! ha! ha! Very good!

Sneer. That, as to comedy, you have not one idea of your own, he believes, even in your commonplace book, where stray jokes and pilfered witticisms are kept with as much method as the ledger of the Lost and Stolen Office.

Sir F. Ha! ha! ha! Very pleasant!

Sneer. Nay, that you are so unlucky as not to have the skill even to steal with taste: but that you glean from the refuse of obscure volumes, where more judicious plagiarists have been before you; so that the body of your work is a composition of dregs and sediments, like a bad tavern's worst wine.

Sir F. Ha! ha!

Sneer. In your more serious efforts, he says, your bombast would be less intolerable, if the thoughts were ever suited to the expression; but the homeliness of the sentiment stares through the fantastic encumbrance of its fine language, like a clown in one of the new uniforms.

Sir F. Ha! ha!

Sneer. That your occasional tropes and flowers suit the general coarseness of your style, as tambour sprigs would a ground of linsey-woolsey; while your imitations of Shakespeare resemble the mimicry of Falstaff's page, and are about as near the standard of the original.

Sir F. Ha!

Sneer. In short, that even the finest passages you steal are of no service to you; for the poverty of your own language prevents their assimilating; so that they lie on the surface like lumps of marl on a barren moor, encumbering what it is not in their power to fertilize!

Sir F. [*After great agitation*] Now, another person would be vexed at this.

Sneer. Oh! but I would n't have told you, only to divert you.

Sir F. I know it—I am diverted—Ha! ha! ha! —not the least invention!—Ha! ha! ha! very good!

Sneer. Yes—no genius! Ha! ha! ha!

Dan. A severe rogue! ha! ha! But you are quite right, Sir Fretful, never to read such nonsense.

Sir F. To be sure—for, if there is any thing to one's praise, it is a foolish vanity to be gratified at it; and if it is abuse—why one is always sure to hear of it from one confounded good-natured friend or another! [*Enter* SERVANT, L.

Serv. Mr. Puff, sir, has sent word that the last rehearsal is to be this morning, and that he'll call on you presently.

Dan. That's true—I shall certainly be at home. [*Exit* SERVANT, L.] Now, Sir Fretful, if you have a mind to have justice done you in the way of answer—Egad, Mr. Puff's your man.

Sir F. Pshaw! sir, why should I wish to have it answered, when I tell you I am pleased at it?

Dan. True, I had forgot that. But I hope you are not fretted at what Mr. Sneer—

Sir F. Zounds! no, Mr. Dangle, do n't I tell you these things never fret me in the least.

Dan. Nay, I only thought—

Sir F. And let me tell you, Mr. Dangle, 't is extremely affronting in you to suppose that I am hurt, when I tell you I am not.

Sneer. But why so warm, Sir Fretful?

Sir F. Gadslife! Mr. Sneer, you are as absurd as Dangle: how often must I repeat it to you, that nothing can vex me but your supposing it possible for me to mind the confounded ridiculous nonsense you have been repeating to me!—And let me tell you, if you continue to believe this, you must mean to insult me, gentlemen—and then your disrespect will affect me no more than the newspaper criticisms —and I shall treat it with exactly the same calm indifference and philosophic contempt—and so, your servant. [*Exit*, L.

Sneer. Ha! ha! ha! Poor Sir Fretful! Now will he go and vent his philosophy in anonymous abuse of all modern critics and authors. But, Dangle, you must get your friend Puff to take me to the rehearsal of his tragedy.

Dan. I'll answer for it, he'll thank you for desiring it. [*Exeunt*, L.

COSTUMES.

MRS. DANGLE.—Plain white muslin morning dress.

DANGLE.—Blue coat; white waistcoat; black pantaloons; black silk stockings; and pumps.

SNEER.—Blue coat, waistcoat, and breeches; silk stockings; pumps; and cocked hat.

SIR FRETFUL PLAGIARY.—Brown coat, with steel buttons; embroidered satin waistcoat; brown breeches; white silk stockings; shoes; buckles; powdered wig and tail; three-cornered hat; lace frill ruffles; and gloves.

THE FATHER'S SACRIFICE.

From Miller's Mahomet.

PERSONS REPRESENTED.

MAHOMET, *the False Prophet.*
ALCANOR, *Chief of the Senate of Mecca.*

SCENE:—*Mecca: A Spacious Grotto.* MAHOMET *discovered with the Alcoran before him.*

Mah. Glorious hypocricy! What fools are they,
Who, fraught with lustful or ambitious views,
Wear not thy specious mask,—Thou Alcoran!
Hast won more battles, ta'en more cities for me,
Than thrice my feeble numbers had achieved,
Without the succor of thy sacred impulse.
[*Enter* ALCANOR.
Why dost thou start, Alcanor? Whence that horror?
Is then my sight so baneful to thee?
Alc. Heavens!
Must I then bear this? Must I meet in Mecca,
On terms of peace, this spoiler of the earth:
Mah. Approach, old man, without a blush; since Heaven,
For some high end, decrees our future union.
Alc. I blush not for myself, but thee, thou tyrant!

For thee, bad man! who com'st with serpent guile,
To sow dissention in the realms of peace;
Thy very name sets families at variance,
'Twixt son and father bursts the bonds of nature,
And scares endearment from the nuptial pillow!
Even truce with thee is a new stratagem.
And is it, insolent dissembler! thus
Thou com'st to give the sons of Mecca peace,
And me an unknown god?

Mah. Were I to answer any but Alcanor,
That unknown god should speak in thunder for me;
But here, with thee, I 'd parley as a man.

Alc. What canst thou say? what urge in thy defense?
What right hast thou received to plant new faiths,
Or lay a claim to loyalty and priesthood?

Mah. The right, that a resolved and towering spirit
Has o'er the groveling instinct of the vulgar.

Alc. Patience, good Heavens! have I not known thee, Mahomet,
When, void of wealth, inheritance, or fame,
Ranked with the lowest of the low at Mecca?

Mah. Dost thou not know, thou haughty, feeble man,
That the low insect, lurking in the grass,
And the imperial eagle, which aloft
Ploughs the ethereal plain, are both alike
In the eternal eye! Mortals are equal:
It is not birth, magnificence, or power,

But virtue only, makes the difference 'twixt them.
Alc. [*Aside*] What sacred truth from what polluted lips!
Mah. By virtue's ardent pinions borne on high,
Heaven met my zeal, gave me, in solemn charge,
Its sacred laws, then bade me on and publish.
Alc. And did Heaven bid thee on, and plunder, too?
Mah. My law is active, and inflames the soul
With thirst of glory. What can thy dumb gods?
What laurels spring beneath their sooty altars?
Thy slothful sect disgrace the human kind,
Enervate lifeless images of men!
Mine bear the intrepid soul; my faith makes heroes.
Alc. Go, preach these doctrines at Medina, where,
By prostrate wretches, thou art raised to homage.
Mah. Hear me: thy Mecca trembles at my name;
If, therefore, thou wouldst save thyself or city,
Embrace my proffered friendship.—What to-day
I thus solicit, I'll command to-morrow.
Alc. Contract with thee a friendship! frontless man!
Know'st thou a god can work that miracle?
Mah. I do—Necessity—thy interest.
Alc. Interest is thy god, equity is mine.
Propose the tie of this unnatural union;
Say, is it the loss of thy ill-fated son,
Who, in the field, fell victim to my rage,
Or the dear blood of my poor captive children,
Shed by thy butchering hands?

Mah. Ay, 't is thy children.
Mark me, then, well, and learn the important secret,
Which I'm sole master of—Thy children live.
Alc. Live!
Mah. Yes—both live—
Alc. What say'st thou? Both!
Mah. Ay, both.
Alc. And dost thou not beguile me?
Mah. No, old man.
Alc. Propitious heavens! Say, Mahomet,—for now,
Methinks, I could hold endless converse with thee,—
Say, what 's their portion! liberty or bondage?
Mah. Bred in my camp, and tutored in my law,
I hold the balance of their destinies;
And now 't is on the turn—their lives or deaths—
'T is thine to say which shall preponderate.
Alc. Mine! can I save them? name the mighty ransom—
If I must bear their chains, double the weight,
And I will kiss the hand that puts them on;
Or, if my streaming blood must be the purchase,
Drain every sluice and channel of my body,
My swelling veins will burst to give it passage.
Mah. I'll tell thee, then; renounce thy pagan faith,
Abolish thy vain gods, and—
Alc. Ha!
Mah. Nay, more,
Surrender Mecca to me, quit this temple,
Assist me to impose upon the world,
Thunder my Koran to the gazing crowd,

Proclaim me for their prophet and their king,
And be a glorious pattern of credulity
To Korah's stubborn tribe. These terms performed,
Thy son shall be restored, and Mahomet's self
Will deign to wed thy daughter.

Alc. Hear me, Mahomet—
I am a father, and this bosom boasts
A heart as tender as e'er parent bore.
After a fifteen years of anguish for them,
Once more to view my children, clasp them to me,
And die in their embraces—melting thought!
But were I doomed or to enslave my country,
Or help to spread black error o'er the earth,
Or to behold these blood-embrued hands,
Deprive me of them both—
—Know me, then, Mahomet,
I 'd not admit a doubt to cloud my choice—
Farewell. [*Exit* ALCANOR.

Mah. Why, fare thee well, then—churlish dotard!
Inexorable fool! Now, by my arms,
I will have great revenge; I 'll meet thy scorn
With treble retribution. [*Exit* MAHOMET.

COSTUMES.

MAHOMET.—Turkish trowsers; tunic bound round the waist with a sash; long outer mantle of yellow striped cloth, reaching almost to the ground, with wide flowing sleeves; turban; long black hair; very full beard; sandals.

ALCANOR.—Turkish trowsers; silken tunic of green; mantle of crimson, with gold or silver embroidery; sandals; scimiter outside of mantle; white hair; long gray beard.

PYRAMUS AND THISBE.

From Shakespeare's Midsummer Night's Dream.

PERSONS REPRESENTED.

NICK BOTTOM, *the Weaver*, (PYRAMUS.)
QUINCE, *the Carpenter*, (PROLOGUE.)
SNUG, *the Joiner*, (LION.)
FLUTE, *the Bellows-mender*, (THISBE.)
SNOUT, *the Tinker*, (WALL.)
STARVELING, *the Tailor*, (MOONSHINE.)
PUCK.

SCENE I:—*A Room in a Cottage at Athens. Enter* SNUG, BOTTOM, FLUTE, SNOUT, QUINCE, *and* STARVELING.

Quince. Is all our company here?

Bottom. You were best to call them generally, man by man, according to the scrip.

Quin. [*Unfolding a paper*] Here is the scroll of every man's name, which is thought fit, through all Athens, to play in our interlude before the Duke and the Duchess, on his wedding-day at night.

Bot. First, good Peter Quince, say what the play treats on; then read the names of the actors, and so grow on to a point.

Quin. Marry, our play is—*The most lamentable Comedy, and most cruel Death of Pyramus and Thisby.*

Bot. A very good piece of work, I assure you, and a merry. Now, good Peter Quince, call forth your actors by the scroll. [*Crossing to* C.] Masters, spread yourselves. [*The rest make room for* BOTTOM.

Quin. Answer as I call you. Nick Bottom, the weaver.

Bot. Ready. Name what part I am for, and proceed.

Quin. You, Nick Bottom, are set down for Pyramus.

Bot. What is Pyramus? a lover, or a tyrant?

Quin. A lover, that kills himself most gallantly for love.

Bot. That will ask some tears in the true performing of it. If I do it, let the audience look to their eyes; I will move storms; I will condole in some measure. To the rest:—Yet my chief humor is for a tyrant; I could play Ercles rarely, or a part to tear a cat in, to make all split.

"The raging rocks,
And shivering shocks,
Shall break the locks
Of prison-gates:
And Phibbus' car
Shall shine from far,
And make and mar
The foolish Fates."

This was lofty!—Now name the rest of the players.—This is Ercles' vein, a tyrant's vein; a lover is more condoling. [*Crosses to* R. *corner.*

Quin. Francis Flute, the bellows-mender.

Flu. (R.) Here, Peter Quince.

Quin. You must take Thisby on you.

Flu. What is Thisby? a wandering knight?

Quin. It is the lady that Pyramus must love.

Flu. Nay, faith, let me not play a woman: I have a beard coming.

Quin. That 's all one. You shall play it in a mask, and you may speak as small as you will.

Bot. An I may hide my face, let me play Thisby, too. I'll speak in a monstrous little voice:—"Thisne, Thisne--Ah, Pyramus, my lover dear! thy Thisby dear, and lady dear!"

[*In a woman's voice. Crosses to* C.

Quin. No, no; you must play Pyramus, and, Flute, you Thisby.

Bot. Well, proceed.

Quin. Robin Starveling, the tailor.

Starve. Here, Peter Quince.

Quin. Robin Starveling, you must play Thisby's mother.—Tom Snout, the tinker.

Snout. Here, Peter Quince.

Quin. You, Pyramus's father; myself, Thisby's father.—Snug, the joiner, you, the lion's part; and, I hope, there is a play fitted.

Snug. Have you the lion's part written? Pray you, if it be, give it me; for I am slow of study.

Quin. You may do it *extempore;* for it is nothing but roaring.

Bot. Let me play the lion, too; I will roar, that I will do any man's heart good to hear me: I will roar, that I will make the Duke say, "Let him roar again: let him roar again."

Quin. An you should do it too terribly, you would fright the Duchess and the ladies, that they would shriek; and that were enough to hang us all.

All. That would hang us, every mothers' son.

Bot. I grant you, friends, if that you should fright the ladies out of their wits, they would have no more discretion but to hang us; but I will aggravate my voice so, that I will roar you as gently as any sucking dove: I will roar an 't were any nightingale.

Quin. You can play no part but Pyramus; for Pyramus is a sweet-faced man; a proper man, as one shall see in a summer's day; a most lovely, gentleman-like man; therefore, you must needs play Pyramus.

Bot. Well, I will undertake it. What beard were I best to play it in?

Quin. Why, what you will.

Bot. I will discharge it in either your straw-color beard, your orange-tawny beard, your purple-in-grain beard, or your French-crown-colored beard—your perfect yellow.

Quin. Some of your French crowns have no hair at all, and then you will play bare-faced.—But, masters, here are your parts; and I am to entreat you, request you, and desire you, to con them by to-morrow night; and meet me in the palace wood, a mile without the town, by moonlight: there we will rehearse; for if we meet in the city, we shall be dogged with company, and our devices known. In the meantime, I will draw a bill of properties, such as our play wants. I pray you, fail me not.

Bot. We will meet; and there we may rehearse more obscenely and courageously. Take pains; be perfect; adieu. [*Exeunt*, D. F.

SCENE II:—*A Moonlighted Wood. Music. Enter* QUINCE, *and his companions.*

Bot. Are we all met?

Quin. Pat, pat, and here's a marvelous convenient place for our rehearsal. This green plot shall be our stage, this hawthorn brake our tiring-house; and we will do it in action, as we will do it before the Duke.

Bot. Peter Quince— [*Crosses to* QUINCE.

Quin. What say'st thou, bully Bottom?

Bot. There are things in this comedy of *Pyramus and Thisby*, that will never please. First, Pyramus must draw a sword to kill himself, which the ladies can not abide. How answer you that?

Snout. By'r lakin, a parlous fear.

Starve. I believe we must leave the killing out, when all is done.

Bot. Not a whit: [*Crosses to* C.] I have a device to make all well. Write me a prologue; and let the prologue seem to say, we will do no harm with our swords, and that Pyramus is not killed indeed: and for the more better assurance, tell them, that I, Pyramus, am not Pyramus, but Bottom, the weaver. This will put them out of fear.

Quin. Well, we will have such a prologue; and it shall be written in eight and six.

Bot. No, make it two more: let it be written in eight and eight.

Snout. Will not the ladies be afear'd of the lion?

Starve. I fear it, I promise you.

Bot. Masters, you ought to consider with yourselves: to bring in, God shield us! a lion among ladies, is a most dreadful thing; for there is not a more fearful wild-fowl than your lion living; and we ought to look to it.

Snout. Therefore, another prologue must tell he is not a lion.

Bot. Nay, you must name his name, and half his

face must be seen through the lion's neck; and he himself must speak through, saying thus, or to the same defect:—"Ladies, or fair ladies, I would wish you, or I would request you, or I would entreat you, not to fear, not to tremble: my life for yours. If you think I come hither as a lion, it were pity of my life: No, I am no such thing: I am a man as other men are;" and there, indeed, let him name his name, and tell them plainly he is Snug, the joiner.

Quin. Well, it shall be so. But there is two hard things: that is, to bring the moonlight into a chamber; for, you know, Pyramus and Thisby meet by moonlight.

Snug. Doth the moon shine that night we play our play?

Bot. A calendar, a calendar! look in the almanac; find out moonshine, find out moonshine.

Quin. Yes, it doth shine that night.

Bot. Why, then may you leave a casement of the great chamber window, where we play, open; and the moon may shine in at the casement.

Quin. Ay; or else one must come in with a bush of thorns and a lantern, and say, he comes to disfigure, or to present, the person of moonshine. Then, there is another thing: we must have a wall in the great chamber; for Pyramus and Thisby, says the story, did talk through the chink of a wall.

Snug. You can never bring in a wall.—What say you, Bottom?

Bot. Some man or other must present Wall: and let him have some plaster, or some loam, or some rough-cast about him, to signify wall: and let him hold his fingers thus; and through that cranny shall Pyramus and Thisby whisper.

Quin. If that may be, then all is well. Come, sit down, every mother's son, and rehearse your parts. Pyramus, you begin. When you have spoken your speech, enter into that brake; and so every one according to his cue.

[*Enter* PUCK, *from behind* L. *unseen.*

Puck. What hempen homespuns have we swaggering here,
So near the cradle of the Fairy Queen?
What, a play toward? I'll be an auditor;
An actor too, perhaps, if I see cause.

Quin. Speak, Pyramus.—Thisby, stand forth.

Pyr. "Thisby, the flowers of odious savors sweet;"—

Quin. Odors, odors.

Pyr. —"Odors savors sweet:
So hath thy breath, my dearest Thisby, dear.—
But, hark, a voice! stay thou but here a while,
And by and by I will to thee appear." [*Exit*, L.

Puck. [*Aside*] A stranger Pyramus than e'er played here. [*Exit*, R.

Flute. Must I speak now?

Quin. Ay, marry, must you; for you must understand he goes but to see a noise that he heard, and is to come again.

This. "Most radiant Pyramus, most lily-white of hue,
Of color like the red rose on triumphant brier,
Most brisky juvenal, and eke most lovely Jew,
As true as truest horse, that yet would never tire,
I'll meet thee, Pyramus, at Ninny's tomb."

Quin. Ninus' tomb, man. Why, you must not speak that yet; that you answer to Pyramus. You speak all your part at once, cues and all.—Pyramus, enter: your cue is past; it is, "never tire."

[*Re-enter* PUCK, *and* BOTTOM *with an ass's head*, L.

This. O,—"As true as truest horse, that yet would never tire."

Pyr. "If I were fair Thisby, I were only thine:"—

Quin. O monstrous! O strange, we are haunted. Pray, masters! fly, masters! help!

[*Exeunt* R. *and* L.

Puck. I'll follow you; I'll lead you about a round. [*Music. Exit*, R. *Re-enter* BOTTOM.

Bot. Why do they run away? This is a knavery of them to make me afear'd. [*Re-enter* SNOUT.

Snout. O Bottom, thou art changed! What do I see on thee? [*Runs off*, R.

Bot. What do you see? you see an ass's head of your own, do you? [*Re-enter* QUINCE.

Quin. Bless thee, Bottom! bless thee! thou art translated. [*Exit.*

Bot. I see their knavery. This is to make an ass of me; to fright me if they could; but I will not stir from this place, do what they can. I will walk up and down here, and I will sing, that they shall hear I am not afraid. [*Sings.*

The oosel-cock, so black of hue,
With orange-tawny bill,
The throstle with his note so true,
The wren with little quill. [*Exit.*

SCENE III:—*A Room in* QUINCE'S *House. Enter* QUINCE, FLUTE, SNOUT, STARVELING, *and* SNUG, L.

Quin. Have you sent to Bottom's house? is he come home yet?

Starve. He can not be heard of. Out of doubt, he is transported.

Flute. If he come not, then the play is marred. It goes not forward, doth it?

Quin. It is not possible: you have not a man in all Athens, able to discharge Pyramus, but he.

Flute. No; he hath simply the best wit of any handicraft man in Athens.

Quin. Yea, and the best person, too: and he is a very paramour for a sweet voice.

Flute. You must say paragon: a paramour is, Heaven bless us, a thing of nought.

Snug. If our sport had gone forward, we had all been made men.

Flute. O, sweet bully Bottom! Thus hath he lost sixpence a day during his life; he could not have 'scaped sixpence a day: an the Duke had not given him sixpence a day for playing Pyramus, I'll be hang'd: he would have deserved it: sixpence a day in Pyramus, or nothing. [*Enter* BOTTOM, L.

Bot. Where are these lads? where are these hearts?

Quin. Bottom! O most courageous day! O most happy hour!

Bot. Masters, I am to discourse wonders; but ask me not what; for, if I tell you, I am no true Athenian. I will tell you every thing right as it fell out.

Quin. Let us hear, sweet Bottom.

Bot. Not a word of me. All that I will tell you is, that the Duke hath dined. Get your apparel together, good strings to your beards, new ribbons to your pumps. Meet presently at the palace; every man look o'er his part; for, the short and the long is, our play is preferred. In any case, let Thisby have clean linen, and let not him that plays the lion, pare his nails; for they shall hang out for the lion's claws. And, most dear actors, eat no onions, nor garlic, for we are to utter sweet breath; and I do not doubt, but to hear them say, it is a sweet comedy. No more words; away! go! away! [*Exeunt.*

SCENE IV:—*Athens: The Palace of Theseus. Enter* QUINCE *as* PROLOGUE, L.

Pro. If we offend, it is with our good will,
That you should think, we come not to offend,
But with good-will. To show our simple skill,
That is the true beginning of our end.

Consider, then, we come but in despite.
We do not come as minding to content you,
Our true intent is. All for your delight,
We are not here. That you should here repent you,
The actors are at hand; and, by their show,
You shall know all that you are like to know.

[*Enter* PYRAMUS *and* THISBE, WALL, MOONSHINE, *and* LION, *as in dumb show*, L.

Pro. [*Crosses to* PYRAMUS] This man is Pyramus;
This beauteous lady Thisby is, certain.
This man with lime and rough-cast, doth present Wall. [*Crossing.*
And this man presenteth Moonshine. [*Crossing.*
By moonshine did these lovers meet
At Ninus' tomb, there, there to woo.
This grisly beast, [*Crossing.*
The trusty Thisby did scare away;
And as she fled her mantle she did fall,
Which lion vile, with bloody mouth did stain:
Anon comes Pyramus, sweet youth and tall,
And finds his trusty Thisby's mantle slain:
Whereat, with blade, with bloody blameful blade,
He bravely broach'd his boiling bloody breast;
And, Thisby tarrying in mulberry shade,
His dagger drew and died. [*Exeunt. Enter* WALL.

Wall. In this same interlude, it doth befall,
That I, one Snout by name, present a wall;
Through which the lovers, Pyramus and Thisby,
Did whisper often very secretly;
And this the cranny is, right and sinister,

Through which the fearful lovers are to whisper.

[*Stands in* C. *of stage. Enter* PYRAMUS, R.

Pyr. O grim-look'd night! O night with hue so black!

O night, which ever art when day is not!
O night, O night! alack! alack! alack!
I fear my Thisby's promise is forgot.
And thou, O wall! thou sweet and lovely wall!
That stands between her father's ground and mine;
Thou wall, O wall! O sweet and lovely wall!
Show me thy chink, to blink through with mine eyne. [WALL *holds up his fingers.*
Thanks, courteous wall: Jove shield thee well for this!
But what see I? No Thisby do I see.
O wicked wall! through whom I see no bliss;
Cursed be thou for thus deceiving me;

[*Enter* THISBE, L.

This. O wall, full often hast thou heard my moans,
For parting my fair Pyramus and me.

Pyr. I see a voice: now will I to the chink,
To spy an I can hear my Thisby's face.
Thisby! [*Peeps through* WALL'S *fingers.*

This. My love! thou art my love, I think.

Pyr. Think what thou wilt, I am thy lover's grace,
O, kiss me through the chink of this vile wall.

[*They kiss through the fingers of* WALL.

This. I kiss the wall, and not your lips at all.

Pyr. Wilt thou at Ninny's tomb meet me straightway?

This. 'Tide life, 'tide death, I come without delay!
[*Exit* PYRAMUS, R., THISBE, L.

Wall. Thus have I, Wall, my part discharged so;
And, being done, thus Wall away doth go. [*Exit.*

[*Enter* LION, *and* MOONSHINE, *with lantern and dog,* L. *They bow, then* LION *takes off his head.*

Lion. You, ladies, you, whose gentle hearts do fear
The smallest monstrous mouse that creeps on floor,
May now, perchance, both quake and tremble here,
When lion rough, in wildest rage doth roar.
Then know that I, one Snug, the joiner, am
A lion fell, nor else no lion's dam:
For, if I should as lion come in strife
Into this place, 't were pity of my life. [*Goes up.*

Moon. This lantern doth the horned moon present.
Myself the man i' th' moon do seem to be.
All that I have to say, is, to tell you, that the lantern is the moon; I, the man in the moon; this thorn-bush, my thorn-bush; and this dog, my dog.
[*Enter* THISBE, L.

This. This is old Ninny's tomb: where is my love?

Lion. Oh—[LION *roars.* THISBE *drops her veil and runs off.* LION *tears veil, and exit. Enter* PYRAMUS, R.

Pyr. Sweet moon, I thank thee for thy sunny beams;
I thank thee, moon, for shining now so bright;
For by thy gracious, golden, glittering gleams,
I trust to taste of truest Thisby's sight.
But stay;—O spite!
But mark,—poor knight.

What dreadful dole is here!
Eyes, do you see?
How can it be?
O dainty duck! O dear!
Thy mantle good,
What! stained with blood?
Approach, ye furies fell!
O fates! come, come;
Cut thread and thrum;
Quail, crush, conclude, and quell! [*Cries.*
O, wherefore, nature, didst thou lions frame?
Since lion vile hath here destroyed my dear:
Which is,—no, no—which was the fairest dame,
That liv'd, that lov'd, that lik'd, that look'd with cheer.
Come, tears, confound;
Out, sword, and wound
The pap of Pyramus:
Ay, that left pap,
Where heart doth hop:—
Thus die I, [*stabs himself*] thus, thus, thus!
Now am I dead,
Now am I fled;
My soul is in the sky:
Tongue, lose thy light!
Moon, take thy flight!
Now die, die, die, die, die!
[*Dies. Exit* MOONSHINE, L. *Enter* THISBE, L.

This. Asleep, my love?
What, dead, my dove?

O Pyramus, arise!
Speak, speak! Quite dumb?
Dead, dead! A tomb
Must cover thy sweet eyes.
These lily lips,
This cherry nose,
These yellow cowslip cheeks,
Are gone, are gone.
Lovers, make moan!
His eyes were green as leeks.
O sisters three,
Come, come to me,
White hands as pale as milk;
Lay them in gore,
Since you have shore
With shears his thread of silk.
Tongue, not a word:—
Come, trusty sword;
Come, blade, my breast imbrue,
And farewell, friends.—
Thus Thisby ends:
Adieu, adieu, adieu. [*Dies.*

COSTUMES.

BOTTOM.—First dress: Gray woolen chiton, without sleeves, reaching to the knees, and fastened round the waist with black belt; flesh-colored arms and legs; shapeless felt hat; short hair; sandals of untanned leather. Second dress: Green armor; helmet; sword.

QUINCE.—First dress: Similar to Bottom. Second dress: Plain black or brown suit.

SNUG.—First dress: As above. Second dress: A lion's mask and skin.

FLUTE.—First dress: As above. Second dress: White linen dress, trimmed with red, and a wreath of red roses.

SNOUT.—Second dress: White shirt, representing a wall.

STARVELING.—Same as first dress of others.

PUCK.—White muslin shirt, trimmed with silver; flesh arms and legs; silvered sandals; silver flowered head-dress; gauze and silver wings.

www.ingramcontent.com/pod-product-compliance
Lightning Source LLC
LaVergne TN
LVHW010220110826
845151LV00004B/1160

9781425526160